TOTAL WAR
AGAINST THE POOR

© 1990 New York CIRCUS Publications, Inc.

New York
CiRCUS
publications, inc.

$7.95   New York, N.Y. ISBN 0-936123-10-9

CONTENTS

Intelligence Conference of American Armies
XVII Conference of American Armies -CEA-

Document III: *Strategy of the International Communism Movement (ICM) in Latin America, Through Various Modes Action*

Accords Approved at the XVII Conference of American Armies

Keeping Control Over Latin America

Epilogue

PREFACE

One of the thorniest problems that has to be confronted by Latin American states hoping to establish democratic governments is the necessity of dealing with the sequel of the political repression carried out earlier by governments of "national security." This is a palpably real problem in countries like Argentina and Uruguay, a problem shaping up as critical in the immediate future of Chile, a problem that someday will have to be dealt with in Guatemala and El Salvador, and just beginning in Peru and Colombia. The presumed peaceful transition from dictatorship to democracy, when it is not mediated by a war that established democratic forces as the victors, gets into great difficulty when it tries to deal with justice, and even when it takes on the simple matter of working out the past. But to paraphrase an old saying, it is surely the case the people who cannot confront their history are condemned to repeat it.[1]

> *- Fr. Ignacio Martin-Baro*
> *Jesuit priest assassinated in*
> *El Salvador, November, 1989*

This is not a usual New York CIRCUS Publications book. A collection of documents coming from a meeting of military personnel throughout the Americas could cause our readership to question our intentions and the direction we are moving. Why is it important for Christians in North America (and elsewhere in the English-speaking world) to read documents from the military? What value do they have in helping us understand our mission with the poor and the oppressed throughout the Americas? Given the changes that have taken place in the world — the melting of the cold-war and the emergence of restricted democracies — have these documents become outdated?

New York CIRCUS Publications was founded to make available to an English-speaking readership documents, reflections, essays and books that would assist in a more complete understanding of the Theology of Liberation and the movement of the Popular Church in the Americas. The editorial line of New York CIRCUS Publications has been to provide primary documents coming both from within the movement, as well as primary documents looking at the ways in which this movement is being attacked. Ways in which the church linked to models for domination responds to this movement for greater democracy within the church — both organizationally and theologically — also have been concerns within the published subject matter of New York CIRCUS Publications.

HISTORICAL CONTEXT

In late 1987 a meeting of military officials from throughout the Americas was held in Mar Del Plata, Argentina. The meeting was held in secret, with no press conferences before or after. The military ideologues and practitioners of the military regimes that have dominated American politics since the mid-60's meet regularly to evaluate their work and project the next phases of their efforts. These same military institutions had met on several occasions to examine their continental efforts to halt progressive movements — carelessly labeled as the International Communist Movement.

Just such shadowy military figures, essentially invisible to the public eye, engineered the coup d'etat in Brazil in 1964; in Uruguay in 1973; in Chile in 1973; in Argentina in 1976. Those from Central America may have included those who worked with the generals who organized the Guatemalan coup d'etat in 1954 or who have been involved in the series of military maneuvers in El Salvador, Honduras, Nicaragua and Guatemala during the last decade. The number present from the U.S. Pentagon remains confidential, as does the exact list of participants. But these kinds of strategy meetings, which have put in motion certain political and military patterns throughout the Americas during the last twenty-five years, undoubtedly have occurred many times.

But there were several things about this meeting that were unique.

First, some of the results of this meeting were leaked to the public. Through a series of maneuvers, the final documents of the conference were made public and circulated as early as December, 1987, throughout North America. In fact, there are some analysts who would go so far as to suggest that a part of the infiltration and subsequent bloody massacre of an Argentina group that led to the Tablada event in January, 1988, was a military response to the leaking of these documents.

Second, the subject matter of these documents is unique. The focus of the new strategy is the church and cultural work. According to the theory of the military analysts, the military war has been won. The guerrilla groups have been contained or destroyed, and the new or remaining danger are those persons or organizations involved in solidarity work, human rights work, religious work among the poor, and cultural work. The documents suggest a far reaching strategy on the part of the military that touches the very social fabric of society throughout the Americas in an effort to complete full and final domination. The reactionary framework for the debate would suggest that this stage comes as the final stage in regaining control of the Americas following the Cuban revolution of 1959, that event which gave birth to the illusory threat of the International Communist Movement in the Americas.

Third, the documents themselves are controversial. Are they real? How authentic are they? There are progressive organizations in the United States which have dismissed these documents as fraudulent. The debate argues that the manner in which they were leaked and the way in which they have been circulated would suggest an overly dramatized and highly isolated confrontation between the ultra-right and the ultra-left. Others would suggest they were leaked by the military themselves as a means for creating the conditions that led up to the assassination of several progressive persons and subsequent raiding of several organizations in Argentina in January, 1988.

A CHURCH UNDER FIRE

What is clear is that the Theology of Liberation and the Church of the Poor are under fire, as are the political projects that would seek a more equitable distribution of the hemisphere's resources, participatory democracy, national sovereignty and models for economic development that take national priorities as their first consideration. The invasion of Panama, the direct North American intervention in the Nicaraguan electoral process through the open funding of opposition parties, and the continued military occupation of Honduras are but the tip of the iceberg of a continental initiative to maintain control of the Americas.

There are those who believe the church -- as an independent social institution, given the autonomy of religion -- is exempt from such attack. There are those who would argue the church is exempt from this struggle within itself, and is no party to such conflicts in the broader society.

Throughout the 1980's, New York CIRCUS Publications opened the debate in the English speaking world by publishing a series of books looking at the neoconservative movement within the United States and its effort to destroy church involvements in progressive issues. These books, by Ana Maria Ezcurra, were also controversial books that were ignored by many progressive church leaders — prior to their early retirement or resignations as the liberal church has moved further and further to the right.

The documents from the military meeting in Argentina give credence to the argument that there is a systematic effort on the part of the forces of domination to intervene in and control the movement of the churches. How else can we understand the assassination of Archbishop Romero and the Jesuits in El Salvador? How else can we understand the arrest and torture of North American priest Jim Carney in Honduras? How else can we understand the movements of the Vatican to control the Theology of Liberation? How else can we understand the return of the Papal Nuncio from the Vatican to Panama a few days prior to the surrender of Manuel Noriega in a U.S. military plane?

The documents that follow must make us think again about the struggles in our hemisphere and the forces that affect and attempt to control progressive movements at this point in history. The reading of these documents dare not de-mobilize us or de-stabilize us, as the enemy would perhaps wish or desire. Rather, the reading and study of these documents must be linked to a deeper analysis on the part of Christians around the world on the role of the church in social movements and the ways in which the dominant forces can use it, attack it, or neutralize it in given historical moments.

For New York CIRCUS Publications, the authenticty of the documents can be seen in the events of the last few years. Beginning with the Santa Fe documents of the early Reagan and early Bush administrations, progressive forces within the religious sector have been singled out as objects for neutralization. The documents from Mar Del Plata are but yet another indication of the sinister way in which this attack against the churches in the Americas is planned and implemented. Historical events give credibility to the authenticity of the material. New York CIRCUS Publications ends this book with a reflection from Pablo Richard, a Chilean theologian, in which he reflects on the meaning of the assassination of the six Jesuits in El Salvador in November, 1989. The perpetrators of this crime remain free. Death threats against those in the church in El Salvador continue. The conscious religious activist needs to examine the Total War Against the Poor in all of its aspects, including the way in which the church is used and attacked to implement a strategy of the rich in the growing gap between the rich and the poor, the North and the South.

*　　*　　*　　*　　*　　*

We are grateful to our German brothers and sisters, who provided the rigorously-documented introductory material which we include in this edition, for their courage and wisdom in publishing this manuscript in German (Totaler Krieg gegen die Armen, Herausgegeben von Ulrich Duchrow, Gert Eisenburger, Jochen Hippler, Munchen: Kaiser Taschenbucher, 1989) and working with us so closely in making the English edition possible. They are indeed a part of a church leadership strengthened by their faith to speak the truth at this point about the nature of the attack on the churches in the Americas. Their truth is not an easy truth to see nor is it easy for American church leadership to perceive.

It is our hope that the publication of these documents can both assist our own church leadership in understanding the world in which we operate, as well as assist Christians in congregations throughout the States in understanding the nature of the struggle of the church throughout the Americas. It is our hope that their publication can indeed assist all of us in our common efforts to demilitarize the Americas in our common pursuit of peace with justice.

As is the usual style of our work, New York CIRCUS Publications is indebted to a number of persons who volunteered their precious time and talents to make this book possible. Translators, editors, word processors and layout personnel are essential for a book like this to become a reality. We would like to give a special word of thanks to the following persons for the generous donation they have made of their time and talents. For the translation work, we are indebted to Cindy Callahan and Christopher Faber. Betsy Shackelford and Elice Higginbotham spent many hours working together to edit this material, attempting to be as faithful as possible to the original text, while making it understandable to English readers. Colette Flanagan, Gregory Quirk and Victor Cole spent many late hours inputing and formatting the material. James Goff was instrumental in making the documents available to us. Finally we must express deep gratitude to the Cadbury Trust for helping to subsidize production of this English edition. May all these hours of dedicated work serve as an example for us as we meet the challenges these documents raise.

New York CIRCUS Publications
New York, New York
September, 1990

---

[1] Martin-Baro, Ignacio. Commonweal, "Reparations: Attention Must Be Paid," pp.184-185, March 23, 1990.

THE DOCUMENTS :

THE (LATIN) AMERICAN MILITARY ALLEGIANCE TO THE ALTERED IMAGE OF THE ENEMY

I. The Documents

The (Latin) American Military Allegiance to the Altered Image of the Enemy

In 1960 a meeting took place, on the suggestion of the USA, in the Panama Canal Zone. It involved the top echelons of the Latin American military and their US counterparts, who gathered to consult on a joint approach to guaranteeing "security" in the Americas. This meeting was a reaction to the success of the Cuban revolution (early January 1959) and at the same time marked the birth of the Conference of American Armies (Conferencia de Ejercitos Americanos, CEA), which has met annually ever since. The main objective of these conferences always has been to discuss and coordinate the combating of uprisings, "subversion" and unrest in Latin America, from a specifically military perspective and under US leadership. For the US armed forces, these conferences were an important opportunity to exert influence on Latin America and its high-ranking officers, backed up by US aid to the Latin American armies in terms of training and equipment. The CEA and its working groups frequently have served to win the allegiance of Latin American military leadership to the respective US strategies for the continent.

In November, 1987, the Conference took place in Argentina. Detailed documentation was brought to the table by the Conference of Intelligence Services of the American Armies (Conferencia de Inteligencia de Ejercitos Americanos, CIEA) and a number of decisions were taken, after due appraisal and analysis by participants. All the material was top secret but was leaked (almost fully) to an Argentinean group (Movimento Todos por La Patria) a year later. The contents of these secret documents are remarkable. While they contain little that specialists did not already know or at least suspect, they are of great value. They reflect the worldview, mentality and strategies of high-ranking US and Latin American officers. Despite Gorbachev and the years of growing divisions within the political left, the documents place terrorist groups, drug dealers and liberation movements on the same footing, seeing them all as "controlled by Moscow." "The worldwide terrorist organizations do not act on their own: on the contrary, they are led and guided logistically by the USSR and its allies forming a true terror international." (CIEA Document I, conclusions This is an attempt to preserve the old bogeyman of world communism, albeit modified: "Eurocommunism" and Gorbachev's policies are seen as attempts to achieve the old goals of world domination by new, more efficient means.

The secret documents are of great political significance in that they generally smear human rights groups, calling them instruments of the "international communist movement." In the context of some of the countries participating in the Conference, this runs very close to outlawing these organizations and placing them in the political – or even military – firing line. The killing of numerous human rights activists, priests, trade unionists and foreign solidarity workers and the existence of death lists in individual countries are too well-known for such attempted defamation to be taken lightly (see e.g. "The Banzer Plan of 1975," in U. Duchrow, Global Economy, A Confessional Issue for the Churches, Geneva, 1987. The documents contained in this volume mention, e.g., Amnesty International, Brot fur die Welt and Adveniat as allegedly supporting the "international communist movement." Smear campaigns against humanitarian and other organizations are just to be understood as part of a broader campaign. They must not be dismissed as individual aberrations and brushed aside.)

Further, the CEA participants suspect the representatives of Theology of Liberation of supporting "subversive" and at times even class them as militant communists. The military and the conservative members of the church hierarchy seek to counteract such tendencies.

One might even claim that the documents reflect with almost unprecedented clarity what could be called the "military-theological complex," by analogy with the term "military-industrial complex." Theology here becomes a tool for a broad based war against social and political changes.

The documents also reveal the great extent to which the Latin American military leadership already have accepted the US strategies of counterinsurgency and low-intensity warfare. Even though the terms are rarely used, the message is clear: military means alone cannot guarantee control over Latin America, but only joint recourse to psychological, economic and political measures.

At many points the analyses of the CEA match the views expressed by the Santa Fe Committee. This offshoot of the rightwing conservative, non-governmental Council for Inter-American Security released a political platform in the USA in 1980 which caused a sensation and became a plank in President Reagan's policy on Latin America. For this reason we shall compare this text below with the Santa Fe II paper of 1988, intended as an updated policy proposal for the Bush Administration. A comparison will reveal the extent to which concepts have been stabilized and consolidated in the last few years, while still being polished and modified in order better to adapt to reality and take account of new experience.

II. Backround: "Total War"

In the Gorbachev age, many old enemy images and political patterns are being shaken up. The "new thinking" in foreign policy has, at least at some points, begun to blur old lines of conflict and attenuate traditional policies of confrontation.

Three questions are increasingly raised. First, what will be the medium and longterm effect of the "new thinking" and new political approach in the Soviet Union on the thought and political praxis in western countries? Will there also be a "new thinking" in NATO, the Federal Republic of Germany, and the USA, taking up the Soviet initiatives and developing them further? Secondly, how stable and durable can the new Soviet approach under Gorbachev be if the West remains caught up on its old thinking? Can a policy of flexibility and accommodation survive in the long run, if it is only pursued by one side? And thirdly, what do these questions mean for the Third World in the so-called North-South conflict?

So far the reactions to Gorbachev in Western Europe and the USA have been, at best, contradictory.

At the beginning of the nineties, then, the world is in a situation in which no accurate assessment can be made of the durability and chances of Gorbachev's foreign policy; likewise, no consistent western response to it is discernible. So the world situation is anything but clear, particularly in the Third World. Speculating about future developments in international relations would thus be extremely risky. The effects of the relationship between the superpowers on the North-South conflict cannot be predicted either. This is why the only remaining option is to take a closer look at the pattern of these relationships up to now. The secret documents published here will assist us greatly in so doing.

This introduction will focus on US policy. The USA is not only still the economically, militarily and politically strongest world power, but also the "leader" of the western alliance and of a considerable part of the Third World. The USA often goes beyond its own national interests to represent "western interests" as a whole, in and toward the developing countries. Finally, precisely for Latin America, it is by far the most important external factor, having exercised inestimable historical influence.

1. System Conflict and Interests

in the Third World

Right at the beginning, CIEA Document I goes to the heart of the matter in the opinion of the military secret services: "the control and distribution of natural resources and strategic raw materials." This being so, the foreign policy coordinates of the USA are defined by three dimensions, independently of the tendency and conceptions of any given administration in Washington:

1. By the relationship with the other most important capitalist countries – Japan, Canada, the European Economic Community (EEC) and a few others (West–West relations). The traditionally very close relations here are being gradually loosened due to increasing economic and trade conflicts, and to political and strategic differences. In these areas, the USA is in a weaker position as compared to the 1950s and 1960s. The need for relatively close cooperation still prevails, otherwise common "western interest" could hardly be pursued effectively (the term "western" is naturally meant in the political and economic sense, not geographically).

2. By the relationship with the Soviet Union and its allies (East–West division). Here, too, the US position has weakened somewhat due to military

and economic changes in the last few decades. At
the same time, this is the field of US foreign
policy that is most ideological (featuring autonomous anti-communist enemy images, which frequently hinder realistic policy-making). The
East-West division contains elements of competition deriving from nation states, but also from
economic policy and military strategy.

3. By the relationship with the Third World (North-
South conflict). From the US standpoint, the most
drastic changes have taken place here in the last
thirty years: the general dominance of the 1950s has
been disrupted politically on several occasions
(starting with the Cuban revolution, then in Iran and
Nicaragua). At the same time some "newly industrialized countries" (NICs) have developed into serious
economic competitors, causing the USA more headaches
than their Japanese or European rivals do. The four
"dragons" of Southeast Asia come to mind, but also
the role of OPEC (Organization of Petroleum Exporting
Countries) in the '70s.

These three problem areas, highly complex in themselves, are so interwoven that US foreign and security policies likewise very complex. Competition with
EEC countries is fought out in the marketplaces of
the Third World (nuclear power plant exports to South
America, agricultural exports to Egypt). Another
example is the massive effect of political and military competition with the Soviet Union and US relations with Third World Countries. So US Third World
policy almost always contains a strong dimension of
West-West and East-West relations.[1]

a) Economic Interests

The USA is the traditional leader of the world economic system dominated by the industrialized countries.
Inexpensive, reliable access to raw materials and
energy sources, plus the Third World as an outlet and

field for investment are important interests, always cited as the motivating factors for US policy. It has already been indicated that it is not merely a matter of bilateral issues between the USA and the Third World. The economic competition with other industrialized countries frequently occurs right at this point. Another oft-cited argument is the alleged interest of the Soviet Union in cutting off the West's sources of raw materials in the Third World (e.g. at the Persian Gulf or in southern Africa).

b) Military and Strategic Interests

The USA has a world wide network of military bases, many of which are in Third World countries like the Philippines, Honduras, Panama, Oman, Egypt, the Caribbean and elsewhere. These bases – and their corresponding communications and transport connections – are extremely important for the projection of US power into certain regions and also for scenarios of a global conflict with the Soviet Union.[2] The Near and Middle East can thus be understood as an extension of the southern flank of NATO, or the shipping lanes through the Caribbean as an essential reinforcement route in the event of a war in Europe or the Middle East. Alongside their back-up function for economic and political interests, these military-type considerations tend to develop a life of their own and to be defended for their own sake.

c) Political Interests

The pursuit of economic and military interests by the USA in the Third World includes a whole package of other interests: stability in certain world regions, stability of friendly governments, accessibility of these countries in political, economic and military terms – all this, in turn, leading to its interest in exerting influence on domestic policy. Ideological dominance of "western values" and economic models geared to a market economy thus seem attractive, as does a general tendency to foster elements of military domination. The combating of any form of socialist, communist or anti-imperialist/nationalist tendency – or whatever can be taken for this – is thus almost automatic: such tendencies reduce the economic, military and political availability of the Third World.

Two supplementary comments are relevant here. First, there is the question of the <u>legitimation</u> of one's own power politics. It is obvious that political forces, including states, never define their selfish interests as such, striving instead for arguments to put them in a good light. Self-interest must be presented such that it is masked by a (fictitious) general interest – only then can it be really effective. The US governments of the '80s put forward a whole set of rationales, resorting to earlier patterns of argument: e.g. combating international communism which allegedly wants to enslave Third World countries and is anti-freedom – an argument dating back to Stalinism and the Cold War. Pursuing US interests is here redefined as the promotion of freedom in the (third) world, e.g. the contras (largely remnants of the old dictatorship) turn into "freedom fighters."[3] Or the securing of access to raw materials and outlets in the Third World becomes securing the "freedom of world trade," which likewise benefits everyone. Other actions are ostensibly to combat terrorism (e.g. the air-raid on Libya) or to free hostages (the invasion of Grenada).

The main legitimation mechanism is still anti-communism. It allows the US government to combat the "Soviet peril" by military means even in places where there cannot be the slightest suspicion of Soviet influence. This is illustrated by the attempt of the CIEA documents to see Soviet agents not only in every liberation movement but also in churches and in solidarity and human rights organizations.

Second, it must be pointed out that the US interest structure outlined above provides a good basis for cooperation with important local elites in the Third World. The military and economically powerful groups in those countries often share the same or similar interests: like the USA, they are mostly interested in "stability" - i.e. retaining their power - and are economically linked with large US corporations. Alternatively, they benefit from US economic and military aid. It is only natural that they should share US anti-revolutionary and anti-communist ideas. The interests of those elites and those of US policy will hardly ever be absolutely identical, yet they generally overlap to a considerable degree and ensure that common plans and strategies are developed to counteract "subversion." The documents published in this volume are a good example of this. In order to understand and analyze these texts one must thus examine the interplay between the complex of US interests in a particular case and the interests of local power elites.

2. Modern Latin American Experience

The history of the USA is a history of expansion, especially on the American continent. The attempt to conquer Canada, the appropriation of Indian territory and the genocide of its inhabitants, the taking of Texas and the war against Mexico with the subsequent annexation of half of its sovereign territory, numerous military interventions in Central and South America, including the (abortive) attempt to introduce slavery to South America and to annex it to the Union at the same time, the acquisition of the land west of the Mississippi from France and of Florida from Spain - all this marked the first century of the new nation. The turn of the century then brought a fresh surge of expansionism: the war with Spain and the dominance over Cuba (including the USA's "right" of military intervention, enshrined in the Cuban constitution) and the control over Panama, to name but two important examples.

This turbulent expansionist urge was only confined by considerations of utility and the limits to US instruments of power.[4]

The 20th century then saw a division of US hegemony regarding Latin America along two main lines. One was the further development of instruments of military repression, e.g. military interventions, or the use of economic and political force and black-mail. The other was the development of what might be termed integrative means of control: the granting of loans and later economic and development aid, technical and military advisors, the formal acceptance of Latin American governments as equals, at least in principle.

On the one hand, there is apparent continuity from President Theodore Roosevelt's policies ("Speak softly and carry a big stick"; "I took Panama") to the interventions in Central America and the Carib-bean in the '20s, to the interventions against Guate-mala (1954), Cuba (1961) and the Dominican Republic (1965), the coup in Brazil (1964) and Chile (1973), and the policies of President Reagan (e.g. the occu-pation of Grenada in 1983 and the indirect war against Nicaragua with the aid of the contras).[5]

On the other, the traditions of integrative means of ensuring control can be traced back in parallel: the "good neighbor policy" of President Franklin D. Roosevelt in the 1930s and early '40s, President Kennedy's "alliance for progress" in the early '60s and President Carter's "human rights policy" from 1977 to 1979.

This is merely a sketchy outline of the two strands of US policy toward Latin America and it may even give the false impression that these policies were contradictory or mutually exclusive. This could easily lead one to personalize one's judgments, comparing "good" presidents (Franklin Roosevelt, Kennedy, Carter) with "bad" ones (Theodore Roosevelt, Eisenhower, Reagan). This would be far from a just appreciation of US foreign policy, however. Both policy strands, the more repressive and the integrative, generally occur together, complementing one another in order to ensure optimum pusuit of US interests. This excludes neither differences in emphasis or accent, nor differences in political rhetoric. Even Franklin Roosevelt did not give up dominance over Cuba: foregoing the Platt Amendment to the Cuban constitution remained extremely half-hearted and purely formal. He terminated the occupation of Nicaragua by US troops, but only after helping to put Somoza's National Guard into power in their place. President Kennedy was not only the president of the Alliance for Progress (a large-scale program of economic and development aid for Latin America) but also the one who applied the most massive repressive strategies of counterinsurgency as a complement to the programs of economic development. Similar evidence could be brought to show the other side of President Carter's human rights policy. And vice versa: presidents usually identified with the repressive form of ensuring control have never disdained to use integrative political instruments if they seemed promising. Just one example of this is President Reagan's pressing for land reform and elections in El Salvador.

This regular linking of integrative and repressive forms of policy is anything by accidental. There are basically two reasons for it. First, both policy strands share the same goal - guaranteeing (or regaining) US interests as outlined above. They aim to secure the accessibility of the countries of Latin America for the USA from an economic, political and military point of view, and hold onto US influence (to the point of dominance, though, if possible, under the threshold of colonial administration). The debate is only on how this can best be achieved. So it is primarily dominated by considerations of utility. Second, all US governments realized – when they were unsuccessful, if not before – that influence and control over Third World countries could be guaranteed only very rarely (or only at intolerable cost) by repressive or integrative means alone. It became clear that neither was really effective without the other.

3. Modern Concepts of Ensuring Control: LIC

The more modern buzzwords in this context are "counterinsurgency" and "low-intensity warfare" or "low-intensity conflict" (LIC). These terms have been intensively discussed since the early '80s, but should not be forgotten that a great upsurge of counterinsurgency began in 1961, at the beginning of the Kennedy presidency, after decades of more improvised activity. Specialized military units were founded, appropriate military doctrines developed and the training and equipment of troops were adapted to new demands. Following the lost Vietnam war in the first half of the '70s counterinsurgency instruments were less active. However, the Reagan Administration, at the start of its term – exactly two decades after John F. Kennedy – immediately picked up on this preparatory work. LIC (counterinsurgency is part of this strategy) owes its emergence to two related ideas:

1. The use of major US troops to control the Third World countries seems a most unattractive option from the US perspective – particularly after Vietnam. Such engagements involve numerous disadvantages. They tie up US troops, logistics, transport capacity etc. for long periods and put them out of action for possibly more "important" situations. NATO would, perhaps, be deprived of

troops, or actions in the Persian Gulf would be hindered. Vietnam had also demonstrated that even an army of 540,000 is no guarantee of success. Vietnam likewise had proven that engaging conventional troops in the jungle (or other difficult terrains) can be quite ineffective against guerilla movements. Finally, major, long-term US military actions in the Third World entail the danger of providing internal resistance; thus foreign policy and military instruments must be restricted to those which will guarantee control while reducing the risk of overt military interventions on any sizable scale.

2. Social upheaval and revolutions in the Third World can rarely be combated by military means alone. Their causes have more to do with social, (world) economic and political problems, with oppression by dictatorships, with intolerable exploitation, etc., than with "Soviet intervention." This insight is also widespread among the US armed forces, even if the "Soviet threat" is always cited as an element of psychological warfare. This is amply proved by internal documents. Hunger, poverty and extreme repression cannot be eliminated by military means, however. The development of instruments to offset the deficiencies of purely military operations thus seems to be urgent. It is no accident that one of the army documents printed here states:

The new concept of the '80s for this purpose is LIC, primarily justified as an appropriate response by the USA to Soviet penetration into the Third World. It is thus, at least in part, a question of superpower rivalry in the Third World. While allied, friendly or client regimes on either side may be involved, or even the superpowers themselves, the term LIC does not mean direct conflict between the USA and the

15

Soviet Union in the Third World. Otherwise one could hardly speak of <u>low</u> intensity conflict. LIC designates conflicts like those in El Salvador and Nicaragua, but also US policy against General Noriega in Panama, the occupation of Grenada and others.[7]

Finally, LIC is not a purely military concept, albeit primarily developed and championed by the US military. It is an integrated political, economic and social approach, supplemented by other psychological, socio-political and diplomatic instruments. It could be generally defined as a more political, integrated policy with military elements, and not a chiefly military concern. William Olson of the US Army War College would concur:

"Indeed, the definition of LIC should not focus on the military level of conflict, but on its political character... The objective is not military conquest but social control, which may use military means as one instrument in its struggle. ... Further use of military force must be measured against its socio-political utility. Military means are a tactical element in a strategic program that emphasizes political goals and means. The use of military power, though essential, is limited, while the use of diplomatic political power may be open ended."[8]

The Field Circular of the US army (FC 100-20) defined low intensity warfare (conflict) in May 1986 as follows:

"Low intensity conflict (LIC) is a limited political-military struggle to achieve political, military, social, economic, or pychological objectives. It is often protracted and ranges from diplomatic, economic, and psychological pressures through terrorism and insurgency. LIC is generally confined to a geographic area and is often characterized by constraints on the weaponry, tactics, and the level of violence. LIC involves the actual or contemplated

use of military capabilities up to, but not including, combat between regular forces."9

This definition consists of two elements. First it explains the general character of LIC, also stressing its civilian aspects (e.g. economic pressure). This is important, as many observers wrongly interpret LIC as being chiefly a military technique. It then explains the specifically military aspects of the concept, i.e. the restricted use of military force.

The definition also makes clear that LIC constitutes a general category to designate differing forms of conflict. The literature accordingly distinguishes between different types of LIC, the most important being:
1. Counterinsurgency, i.e. putting down uprisings.
2. Counter-operations, i.e. organizing subversion and uprisings.
3. Counterterrorism, likewise an umbrella term for very differing instruments and conceptions, which aim at an offensive, military combating of terrorism.
4. Narrowly confined, often "surgical" operations of a conventional military kind. This category can be within one of the three points mentioned above, or independently of them.
5. Other operations, e.g. rescue operations, sending peace-keeping troops etc.10

a) Why Low-Intensity Warfare?

The official US rationale for LIC is interesting. It is claimed that there is stability in the US-Soviet strategic military situation, particularly in the Mediterranean. The Soviet Union can gain nothing by a direct attack on the USA or its NATO allies and thus tries to strike at and encircle the leading capitalist states via the "detour" of the Third World

where numerous conflicts can be "exploited." Secretary of State Schultz once called this a "flanking
maneuver."[11] This argument contains two interesting
components: first, the implicit (and occasionally
also explicit) premise that the USSR is not superior
to NATO in terms of nuclear and conventional weapons,
except in special cases; second, it is thus shifting
to the Third World, instead of confronting the US in
the Mediterranean. This follows from the fact that
the strategic situation in Central Europe is considered stable in the medium and long term, and that
the main threat to western interests today comes from
the Third World, in the US view. This pattern of
argument has not been taken seriously by official
policy makers in the Federal Republic of Germany, nor
by the West German peace movement.

"Consequently, the most likely threats to US interests may arise from local and regional conflicts and
internal instability of US allies or clients.
Morocco, Sudan, Egypt, Israel, Saudia Arabia, Mexico,
Pakistan, the Phillipines, and the Republic of Korea
- American or Western allies to some degree - are all
vulnerable to attack. ... direct attack by an
external enemy is usually the least likely threat.
Internal instability, possibly leading to revolution,
is a more conceivable scenario in many of these
countries."[12]

It was also clear to US military planners that conflicts in the Third World generally are closely
related to deficiencies in the internal development
of these nations. John O. Marsh declared: "If one
studies the regions where there are insurgencies, one
cannot fail to be struck by th ecommonality of the
situations: immature governments, developing economies, exploding populations, and social problems that
relate to inadequate diet, poor health care, and a
high degree of illiteracy. These uprisings often
occur in areas that are rich in natural resources of
considerable interest to the West. Many of these

governments are susceptible to infiltration, subversion, and destabilization."13

So from the US perspective, the great importance for the capitalist states of certain Third World regions, and their accompanying instability, constitute a central problem for western foreign and security policies. Given the "nuclear impasse" between the superpowers – to quote an official document of the US army – their confrontation is shifting to the Third World and "serve to confine the confrontation to low to mid intensity conflicts within Third World countries, such as Afghanistan and Vietnam, or support for third parties against clients of the other..."14

Thus, LIC seems to be a reaction to the strategic stalemate between the superpowers which makes direct confrontation too risky and un-feasible, and an extension of the conflict into the Third World. Responsibility for these tendencies is quite often attributed to the Soviet Union, which is said deliberately to use LIC strategies as forms of warfare against the USA at a low level, in order to deter the latter from a flexible or massive response.

From the US standpoint, LIC is neither harmless nor insignificant. Instead it is, in practice, a Soviet strategy to wage a global war against the USA without the latter noticing. Former Defense Secretary Caspar Weinberger expressed this view with particular clarity. Early in 1986 he organized a conference on LIC, stating: "The world to day is at war. It is not global war, though it goes on around the globe. It is not war between fully mobilized armies, though it is no less destructive for all that (...) Tonight, one out of every four countries around the globe is at war. In virtually every case, there is a mask on the face of war. In virtually every case, behind the mask is the Soviet Union, and those who do its bidding."15

The assumption that the US military is poorly equipped for LIC engagements naturally implies that "lower" and "higher" intensity wars differ not only in extent but in <u>quality</u>. It is not a matter of "large-scale" or "small-scale" wars, but of totally different types of conflicts. The difference is, for example, that the "high intensity" wars have a conventional military and/or nuclear component, and that they depend on annihilation capability, fire-power, technological standard and related variables. To simplify somewhat: these characteristics are often relatively secondary in the case of "low intensity" conflicts, so that the classical rules of warfare are only of limited use. Medium and high intensity conflicts aim for the military destruction of the adversary's forces and/or territorial gains (or defense). In LIC situations adversarial troop concentrations are the exception – either because they do not exist at all and operations take place only in small groups, or because they cannot be perceived or attacked. So fire-power is secondary. Air force General Cardwell rightly pointed out that, "To deal with this conflict, military planners had to shift from thinking in these terms of conventional nuclear, attrition modeled, technology intensive warfare to one of unconventional, socio-political, protracted and labor intensive warfare. This means that we must shift from the normal way we prepare plans – based upon large forces that relied upon technology to fight the <u>battle</u> – to looking at planning from a more narrow focused perspective – based upon long term, small battles, which may not rely upon attrition nor technology. The aim is no longer to gain and hold territory, but to maintain political and economic access to the thirld world by preempting the Soviets from achieving their expansion aims." [16]

LIC situations are generally strongly political in nature, e.g. the proverbial struggle for the hearts and minds of a civilian population in counterinsurgency campaigns. This in itself indicates that troops trained for tank battles in Fulda Gap or for

nuclear war would not necessarily be useful in LIC situations.

(The above-mentioned "surgical" operations, precise, rapid strikes with conventional means, constitute a special case. For this reason, many officers do not regard them as LIC operations at all. Yet they are used as elements of LIC warfare, not necessarily fulfilling a purely military function. Their role can be primarily psychological, propagandistic, economic, or to make a political point. One example might be the mining of Nicaragua's harbors from January to April, 1984, or the air-raid on Libya in March and April, 1986.)

b) Counterinsurgency and Counter-Operations

The political character of LIC becomes particularly clear when one takes a closer look at its individual elements.

<u>Counterinsurgency</u> is a form of conflict that aims primarily at forestalling or preventing open civil war, uprising or similarly (para)military conflict. If incipient uprisings in Third World countries could be quashed purely or primarily by military means, a counterinsurgency campaign would be superfluous. Its very existence is an indication of the political (and socio-political/economic) character of the conflict, an admission that would make a "military solution" either impossible or unacceptably expensive. Counterinsurgency first aims at gaining control over the population, all other aspects – even the direct, military confrontation of guerilla warfare – being in principle subordinate and instrumental to this end. [17]

Counterinsurgency aims at two related goals: first, the remodelling (and "modernization") of a Third World society and its state system according to criteria that made the latter "functional" and also guarantee US control. Second, it aims at separating guerilla movements (or other forms of fundamental opposition) from the population, either through political and economic incentives and/or through military pressures and geographical division. These tasks are obviously not "classical" military actions. This is also the reason why counterinsurgency requires stronger elements of economic aid, development aid, psychological back-up and diplomatic initiatives.

We must not overlook the military aspect of these attempts to "reform," "modernize" and so stabilize a modified, functional status quo. Often these campaigns have to be carried out on the context of escalated civil wars. Frequently the military of the client state becomes the driving force of the operation, with the US military taking on key advisory and training functions. The US military participates to a certain extent in the military conflicts and also in civic action, i.e. projects to promote the infrastructure or support the population (e.g. drilling wells, medical aid etc.) At the same time the different political and economic schemes can only be carried out if the country can achieve a minimum of "security." Military operations and techniques naturally take on great importance in this context.

Over all, it is clear the LIC campaigns by the USA — here in the case of counterinsurgency - have no chance without active back-up by organizations in the respective target country. In concrete terms, without the active and largely competent cooperation of Latin American armed forces, which have to guarantee the repressive consolidation and advancement of the "modernizing" and "civic" elements of the strategy, successful counterinsurgency efforts would hardly be possible in Latin America. [18] This explains the great importance of US aid in training Latin American officers and also of such institutions as the Conference of the American Armies. The present documents illustrate the extent to which the Latin American military have accepted at least the general conception of the US LIC doctrines.

One strategic problem of counterinsurgency often consists in the fact that military, repressive elements may get in the way of the development-oriented elements, and vice versa. [19]

Since counterinsurgency - either preventive or full-scale - mainly aims at the hearts and minds of a population, intensive use is made of forms of psychological warfare. The discrediting of human rights organizations, the persecution and oppression of churches in solidarity activities with the poor, or the instrumentalization or artificial creation of religious organizations, belong to the standard repertoire, as does the frequent resorting to instruments of anticommunist slander. Humanitarian relief organizations or basic communities are transformed - in a flash - into "communist agents" which have to be crushed.

Common instruments now include campaigns associating guerilla movements or undesirable governments with the drug trade in order to smear them. However, as a rule, exclusively politically motivated accusations are levelled in the context of psychological warfare. If governments or organizations supporting the USA are in fact involved in drug trafficking - e.g. important contra leaders in Nicaragua, General Noriega of Panama, when he was on the CIA payroll, or the Afghan Mudjahedin, major heroine dealers in the Afghan-Pakistan border area - this hardly ever has hindered the USA from giving them support.

A further element of psychological warfare is the terrorism charge, again deliberately raised exclusively against political opponents, notable in a big way against liberation movements. For example, El Salvador's FMLN, the PLO in the Middle East and the South African ANC are said to be "terrorist" organizations, while bombing, torture, the shooting of prisoners and other atrocities of the contras or the Mudjahedin have never called forth such a judgement from the USA.

Counterinsurgency operations are not primarily military in character either, although they may appear so at first sight. The best known and, so to speak, "classic" case is the US government's 1981 reorganization of the former National Guard of the Somoza dictatorship into combat troops against Nicaragua. This did not aim at the direct, military ousting of the Nicaraguan government by the contras, nor at invading Managua. They were never in a position to do this and that was not their function. In terms of LIC, the Reagan administration was concerned about achieving a whole package of objectives: military pressure and threat, the economic downfall of Nicaragua through the war and the necessary allocation of resources for defense, the hardening of the internal situation and heightening of internal repression, in sum, the creation of conditions to **destabilize** the Nicaraguan government and the Sandinista revolution. So the main objective of the strategy was the attempt to deprive the government of the loyalty of the mass of the population. Through a coordinated package of military, economic, political, diplomatic and psychological pressure, the internal situation was to be rendered so tense that the Sandinista revolutionary model would not have a chance — yet without running the risk of a direct US intervention. The contra campaign was a central element of this strategy but not a purely military one. The war waged by the contras pursued economic and psychological goals, rather than merely military ones. It aimed to create conditions enabling the downfall of the Sandinista government, without directly bringing this about itself.[20]

Counter operations were specifically legitimized and publicized by the administration, the so-called "Reagan doctrine" postulating the right and duty of the USA not just to stop the expansion of the Soviet Union and the "totalitarian threat" it incorporated (which was one of the aims of counter-insurgency) but, wherever possible, to officially roll back the sphere of Soviet influence in the Third World. To this end, it is legitimate and necessary to give military support to anti-communist "liberation movements" (like the Nicaraguan contras, the Angolan UNITA and the Afghan Mudjahedin).[21] In connection with this ideological legitimation, the USA stages international disinformation campaigns on the state of these societies.

c) The Military Aspect of LIC

So far the primarily political character of LIC has been stressed several times. In order to avoid misunderstandings, however, a number of remarks are necessary.

First, it should be pointed out that neither LIC, nor its precise direction in the US government or the armed forces, is undisputed. To date, LIC is anything but a unified, closed concept. One point at issue is the military emphasis of LIC.

Second, it can also be claimed that the non-military priorities of LIC under the Reagan Administration frequently ended up being proclaimed but not implemented. The priority of the political LIC approach is often not maintained and a creeping militarization of the LIC concept is uncontested. There are arguably two reasons for this: first, the fact that simple "military solutions" for complex problems belonged to the traditional Reagan philosophy, somewhat "refined" during his government but not basically changed. A "political" accept for LIC has clear overtones of Carterism and would be easy to combine with Carters's human rights policy.[22] It thus contradicts the political instincts of many Reaganites (e.g. when land reform in El Salvador is labelled "communist"). In addition, many US officers have raised clear objections to the civic elements of LIC (occasionally also to the military ones), as they do not match their training, experience, ideology and qualifications.

In short, certain postulates of a political (including economic, social policy etc.) emphasis are not used consistently and military means are stressed more instead.

Finally, it should not be forgotten that even within political LIC programs the military aspect is of great and essential importance. LIC does not mean replacing "military" solutions by "political" ones, but rather the removal of the distinction between "military" and "civic." Such clearly "non-military" actions as strikes and demonstrations can, in LIC situations, be understood as "acts of war," while the military can indeed be occupied with medical care of a village population or setting up of infrastructure (civic action). In this sense, civic practices are totally militarized under LIC conditions, while military activities are totally politicized, so that there is hardly any point in comparing them. Military or non-military action undertaken by the armed forces (of the USA and/or a local government) will, however, be of crucial importance for each LIC program. The provision of military and police "security" is also a variable without which every pacification program is bound to fail.

By their very nature, LIC operations cannot be compared with conventional military operations (see above). So it is not surprising when regular military units are not optimally trained and equipped for these functions – this in fact brings us back to the starting point of the whole discussion on low intensity warfare. The most able units in unconventional operations and LIC are the special operations forces (SOF) with their three types of weapons. After the Reagan administration took office they were considerably expanded and equipped with additional equipment and weapons suited to their tasks. A survey of the SOF as a key military instrument of LIC has been given elsewhere.[23]

d) LIC as Psychological Warfare

An important additional aspect is the relationship between US foreign policy and the internal situation. A high-ranking Pentagon official once said: "One of America's most important foreign policy problems is that, since Vietnam, war in the Third World is not allowed."[24]

This is a fundamental hinderance to action on the basis of US foreign policy; not only are specific military options prevented, but the threat of major military operations loses credibility. LIC is seen as the attempt to find a way out of this difficulty. LIC is, after all, a mode of combat that the USA could maintain for years in a given Third World country without arousing any particular public attention. Criticism can be reduced to a minimum, it is thought. The relatively slight US engagement of personel and material would hardly allow for the development of political opposition, let alone a polarization of US society as at the end of the Vietnam war.
"Popular support is not absolutely essential, but there must be at leat benign indifference, especially on th epart of the mass media. Otherwise, Congress

will feel compelled to end U.S. involvement, regardless of the stakes. If LIC can be kept controlled at the lower levels of violence with very little carnage for the TV cameras, then possibly public support, and as a minimum, benign indifference will accrue. Something so pedestrian as Internal Defense and Development, especially when it is relatively successful, will never make the 6 o'clock news."[25]

This argument can be substantiated by the facts. When the USA conducts LIC campaigns in two or three dozen Third World countries at the same time, mostly grouped around economic and military aid programs and usually avoiding the deployment of combat troops, public attention is distracted and easier to contain than in the case of direct, spectacular interventions by the USA, using considerable troop capacity and with corresponding losses, as in Vietnam.

The time factor also plays a role in LIC campaigns. In the case of direct military interventions on a major scale, domestic opposition usually mounts as time goes on; but it is easy to get used to the less spectacular LIC operations. For example, the counterinsurgency campaign in El Salvador, a highly controversial undertaking in 1981-83, was broadly accepted by Congress in 1985-1987. The reasons were certain political and military successes of the campaign, and the fact that it had been possible to avoid the direct military intervention so feared by critics.

What looks like "low intensity" from the perspective of the strong West is enormously intense for the poor populations of the South, where it oppresses and kills. Think of the open conflicts in Nicaragua, El Salvador, the Philippines and southern Africa. Here the people experience LIC directly as "death squads," "contras" and "vigilantes" supported directly by the USA or its allies in their role of intimidation and murder. However, since LIC is not merely overtly

violent but also subtly using economic destabilization and bribery, political pressure and propaganda,
the oppressive intensity goes further and deeper.
When people are subjugated, they are either equipped
with economic privileges or kept so downtrodden that
they are discouraged from working for economic and
social justice and political participation at all.
They are thus the target of a mixture of repressive
measures which many cannot see through and positive
incentives (carrot and stick) to make them accept the
status quo. In South Africa this is called "snaky
repression."

It is essential to break the resistance in people's
hearts, i.e. to pursue ideological combat.

III. The Ideological Target: The Church
of the Poor, International Human Rights
and Solidarity

1. The Struggle between the "Good"and the "Evil" Empire
and the Capitalist Reinterpretation of Democracy

At the end of the '70s there was a clash between two
different emphases in the LIC strategy. On the one
hand, the Carter administration and its ideological
supporters tried to win the hearts and minds of
different target groups in the Third World by publi-
caly supporting those struggling for social justice
in the human rights arena and withdrawing support
from – at least some – overtly repressive regimes.
In this way it was hoped to stabilize societies in
the Third World rent by social tension. This was a
pragmatic, socially technocratic approach, also supported by military officers and their advisors and
sympathetic politicians, weakening as it did the
social base of the guerilla movements in the population.

In contrast to this integrative approach, however, in
the prelude to the Reagan era, a sharp polarizing

emphasis was given the LIC strategy, emphasizing the East-West division. Latin American policy was thus forged out of a meld of classical power and dominance policy and hardline, militant anticommunism. UN Ambassador Jeane Kirkpatrick and the Santa Fe Committee of the Council for Inter-American Security were particular representatives of this orientation. "Foreign policy is the instrument by which peoples seek to assure their survival in a hostile world. War, not peace, is the norm in international affairs... America's basic freedoms and economic self interest require that the United States be and act as a first rate power. The crisis is metaphysical. America's inability or unwillingness either to protect or project its basic values and beliefs has led to the present nadir of indecision and impotence." Thus begins the Santa Fe I document.[26] According to it, war with the aim of making the USA the number one world power again is not a normal struggle for power but a fight to protect the West's basic values and beliefs. It is war in the context of a metaphysical crisis.

"The war is for the minds of mankind" (p. 32). "The United States should promote a policy conducive to private capitalism, free trade and direct local and foreign investment in productive enterprises in Latin America" (p. 33) Hence the Santa Fe Committee's suggestion that the "United States initiate an economic and ideological campaign by ...., above all, providing the ideal behind the instrument of foreign policy through education programs designed to win the minds of mankind. For the belief behind the policy is essential to victory; and the United States is engaged in World War III" (p. 52).

The theology behind this dualistic world view is a reinterpretation of the last chapters of the Revelation of St. John (14 ff.). The military power of the USA identifies itself here with the angels which cast down the hostile powers at the Last Judgement, in order to help to bring about the Kingdom of God by means of the "thousand years' reign" (with the eschatological events here being interpreted as a normal state of affairs in terms of social Darwinism). The military can thus see itself as part of salvation history, as the armed hand of God. On the other side is the Soviet Union, identified with the kingdom of Satan. Whoever combats and casts down communism will be pleasing unto God. President Reagan's statement that the Soviet Union was the "evil empire" was not a slip of the tongue. It expressed the thinking of a broad front of the New Right, comprised of different religious groupings. It ranges from the new charismatic groups like the Neopentecostalists to the traditional Roman Catholic groups of the Cross and Sword alliance. The charismatic grouping has become known through the tele-evangelists of the electronic churches who are flooding America, both North and South. There are shattering witnesses to this combination of dualistic piety and military cruelty. Clemente Diaz Aguilar, for example, reports that in 1983, in Guatemala, he was tortured by members of one of the Neopentecostalist churches because they took him for a liberation theologian. General Rios Montt, then president of Guatemala, was himself a Neopentacostalist. When it turned out that the torturers had mistaken Diaz Aguilar for someone else, they said, "Brother, we're Christians too and we beg your pardon but we are acting on orders from our superiors...and, as you know, we're fighting communism, which is the devil himself."[27] Another pastor received similar treatment in 1982. His torturers told him, "Rios Montt has said that there are subversive types among the pastors and they have to be exterminated, pastor or not. The root of the evil is the demon in them, which makes them into communists." "Well," the pastor continued his report, "He actually did say that at a radio and TV press conference. Then he was asked, 'Is it true that you kill Indians' And he answered, 'I don't kill Indians, just communist demons. I send Indians to heaven, that's all'."[28]

31

The medieval, inquisitorial variation of this military, theological dualism was witnessed in 1987 in Argentina when the military rebelled under Mohamd Ali Seineldin. A document based their mission on fighting subversion through a long historical survey ranging from Revelation, Augustine's "two kingdoms," and the medieval crusades and heretic hunts, to the struggle against communism.[29]

All this may sound strange, but in the USA it is supported by many research institutes and organizations, financed to the tune of millions by industry, banks or the government. Their aim is to produce theology and ideology for capitalism and, under the guise of anticommunism, for the fight against social change. The Institute for Religion and Democracy (IRD) is particularly well known.[30]

What was characteristic of the Reagan period was the combination of the LIC tendencies mentioned earlier – that of "winning hearts and minds," and the more strictly confrontational. Although a certain tension, never entirely resolved, existed between them (one being more zealously ideological and other more "enlightened" and pragmatic) there was little friction in their interaction. The connecting link was the recognition that low intensity warfare in the Third World is an all-out war at the social grassroots, involving all aspects of society. This was attractive for anticommunist ideologues since it indicated great determination, and also for practical souls who assumed, in any case, that military or economic means alone would not suffice to "liberate" a Third World country. This "total war" could thus be waged against the Soviet Union and its "henchmen," worldwide communism, terrorism or authentic, local guerilla movements, or against general "destabilizing" conditions – it was only a matter of personal and political inclination.

This of course blurs the distinctions between war and peace, violence and politics, civic, religious and military. Strikes and fliers are redefined as "acts of war," the granting of loans, e.g. by the World Bank, is interpreted as "relevant to war" and ideological or religious conflicts are understood from the angle of psychological warfare. The human rights situation in a country is only perceived as a variable of public relations or relative to its stabilizing or destabilizing effect, and the economic or social position of people only from the angle of their repercussions on stability. So it is no wonder that organizations which, on principle, work for improved human rights, social reforms and participation by the population in political processes are regarded with mistrust and even combated. Anything not fitting into LIC policy is seen as a disturbing or hostile element and treated accordingly.

This finding is again fully confirmed by the second Santa Fe documnet: "A Strategy for Latin America in the Nineties," is designed to lay down policy for President Bush.[31] The Santa Fe Committee has toned down considerably the apocalyptic, metaphysical overtones of the 1980 paper, instead supplying an exposition of the ideology of "democratic capitalism," unambiguous in its clarity. That is of great value for understanding the CIEA secret documents, which only indicate at different points that the values to be defended against "communist subversion" are "democratic, capitalist" in nature, without further elaboration. So what are the highest values necessitating an total war?

The US goal in Latin America, and thus the content of capitalist democracy, is clearly defined as free enterprise, a free capital market and then an economy free of political control, "... to move Latin societies toward democratic capitalism - that is, free-enterprise systems and national capital markets which sustain independent societies" (p. 15). The core of the proposed economic strategy is thus national capital markets, deregulation and privatization. (p. 35)

What does political democracy mean in this context? Here we are instructed that, in the West, we have so far looked too much to elected governments because they are only temporary (p. 5). A "democratic regime" also entails permanent government, however, i.e. institutional structures and bureaucracies like the military, the police and the judiciary, along with civic administration. They are there to pre-serve the "independence of society," i.e. fundamenta-lly the system of free enterprise and the capital market. Just as the Soviets strive for control of the military in other countries, the USA must do this just as realistically (p. 9). Above all, however, it must take up the struggle for culture and values (p. 10ff).

It thus comes as no surprise to read the concrete proposals to strengthen what is here called "demo-cracy" (p. 11ff): 1. influencing the bureaucracies, the military and political culture; 2. oppressing parties that do not share this notion of capitalist democracy; 3. strengthening these values in the military through the International Military Education and Training (IMET) program; 4. strengthening the police and judiciary. Democracy, equated as free capitalism, is thus to be promoted precisely through the strengthening of repressive institutional mea-sures.

One element still needs to be mentioned in order to see how this ideology of capitalist democracy aims at the long-term safeguarding of the profits of trans-national capital with the aid of the US leadership. Santa Fe II accuses the Reagan Administration of "failure to use the debt crisis to create healthy capital markets" (p. 15). The suggested way to do this is the aggressive promotion of debt/equity swaps to encourage growth of the private, productive sector. What is meant by this? The swaps mean turning debts into shares in national means of production. Foreign or local companies buy, for example, 50 million dollars in debt from a US bank for 25 million, but are paid 50 million in local currency by the central bank of the debtor country on condition that it is productively invested. Joint ventures are particularly desired between US and national capital, in order to minimize nationalism, that is, the countries' controlling their industry themselves. In this way US capital keeps a grip on national economies and uses the debt crisis to invest 100 percent for 50 percent of the cost.

This very subtle policy of economic, political and military control can easily be put across ideologically, under the banner of freedom, democracy and religion. Only on closer inspection does one see that "freedom" means the freedom of industrial and financial capital, untrammelled by political considerations in the sense of concern for the common good, and thus particularly profitable. What is meant by "democracy" is the focus on strengthening the military, police, judiciary and propaganda; by religion, the blessing of this policy. One only realizes all this on hearing the cries of victims of the "transnational capitalism of (trans)national security."[32]

2. The Church of the Poor and Liberation Theology

A church and theology contradicting this policy for the sake of God and humankind can only be combatted as a communist enemy by the policy's defenders. The Santa Fe Committee defined the problem and the task of the USA as follows: "US foreign policy must begin to counter (not to react against) liberation theology as it is utilized in Latin America by the liberation theology' clergy. The role of the church in Latin America is vital to the concept of political freedom. Unfortunately, Marxist-Leninist forces have utilized the church as a political weapon against private property and productive capitalism by infiltrating the religious community with ideas that are less Christian than Communist" (p. 20). Santa Fe II defined the Theology of Liberation in similar terms: "It is a political doctrine disguised as religious belief having an anti-Papal and anti-free enterprize meaning in order to weaken society's independence from states control" (p. 11). So the western cultural assets to be protected from the Theology of Liberation are the Pope and capital kept clear of the interests of the common good!

The secret documents presented in this book identify the Theology of Liberation, the Church of the Poor and international solidarity and human rights groups as the chief ideological enemy in the present phase of the war by the USA for the cause of capitalism and world hegemony. This must be seen in the whole context of US interests. The above-mentioned groups represent opposing forces to the present economic, social and ecological exploitation concerned for the "control and distribution of natural resources and strategic raw materials." The US efforts to maintain dominance in the Third World and worldwide, in the framework of the transnational capitalist system, and also to include the changing commitment of the churches in its sights, represent a long story that begins many years before the Santa Fe documents. The Rockefeller Report on the Americas[33] is of basic significance here. In 1969, Governor Nelson Rockefeller, at the request of President Nixon, set off with a group of advisors to travel through twenty countries of Central and South America in order to assess the whole situation on behalf of US interests. The resulting book, in the section entitled "The Cross and the Sword" (p. 31ff) of tendencies in the Latin American church and military which were worrysome for the USA. He observed that the church and military hierarchies stemming traditionally from the well-to-do classes were being infiltrated by members of the working class and poor classes of the population, and were in some cases calling for social change and justice. To counter this tendency, the report suggests the expansion of US military training for Latin American officers in Panama and the USA, in order to commit the military to the "American way of life." With respect to the church in Latin America, the US State Department commissioned the Rand Corporation to conduct a study on "Latin American Institutional Development: The Changing Catholic Church."[34]

This study bore the imprint of the dramatic changes brought to the Latin American churches by the Second Vatican Council and the consequent declaration of the Conference of Latin American Bishops in Medellin (1968).[35] The chief criterion of judgement is anticommunism. Up until the late fifties, anticommunist strategies in the church were noted; but a "relaxation of systematic anticommunism" occurred in the late sixties. A further reason for concern, according to the study, was a growing nationalism within the Latin American church. The latter was turning against US imperialism, seeing that Vatican II itself had condemned under-development and imperialism.

This Rand Corporation study, from a body traditionally sympathetic to the Pentagon, undertook a very detailed analysis and assessment of church and theological developments - clearly with the goal of detecting the weak points so as to tackle the change. The following elements were included: the church had institutional interests and could thus not go along with the radical demands for justice of Christian Base Communities, having instead to seek arrangement with the state; the church was thought to be divided in itself; alongside the new tendencies, rightwing forces continues; and many people in the middle did not know what the conflict was all about. The document thus cherished the hope that, as long as violent revolution could be prevented, the churches would again turn from practical support for change to another general condemnation of wrongdoing (p. 11).

Moreover, the reaction against individual priests and lay people who speak out too strongly for social justice was revealed in 1972 in the so-called Banzer plan:[36] active Christians were isolated, slandered and, if necessary, assassinated.

Since 1969 there have been many other documents besides those mentioned, and also a flood of books, publications, TV campaigns, etc., in order to combat the theology of liberation and its supporters in the church.[37]

The new elements in the secret documents published here can be summarized as follows:

1.   In earlier analyses the chief concern was the changed attitude of the Vatican in the period during and after Vatican II.   Church groups calling for social justice could then appeal to the supreme church authority for support.   This changed when John Paul II took office, and appointed Cardinal Joseph Ratzinger as head of the Sacred Congregation for the Doctrine of Faith, to the apparent glee of the military.   The enemies of the socially committed part of the church now could turn for support to the supreme doctrinal authority of the church.[38]

The military secret services used Cardinal Ratzinger's same line of argument exactly in the third CIEA document, in the two statements of the Theology of Liberation.[39]   Liberation theology is all right as long as it relates to "actual" church concerns, i.e. pastoral care, and leaves aside "secular" social problems. That means that the Theology of Liberation is no longer totally rejected, at least the term is accepted (it is too well founded biblically to reject).   Yet the concept can be reinterpreted, tamed, so that God is only directly connected with

"spiritual" things and not with the structural matters of political economy.

Anyone who directly relates God with economic and
social structures, on the other hand, is dubbed a
moderate or radical Marxist and communist. On this
basis, critical social scientists, theologians and
Base Communities using these fundamental social or
political criticisms for theological reasons are
defined as being outside the church.

Biblical theology now has universally recognized that
the Theology of Liberation is right in assuming - on
the basis of the Exodus and the freeing of the slaves
from Egyptian oppression (Exodus 3 ff) - that the God
of Israel gives priority to the poor and weak, and
saves them. In the eyes of the military, the representatives of the "preferential option for the poor"
are heretics for whom the church can no longer give
backing. However, under the state of war in which
the well-to-do and powerful involved the majority of
people in the impoverished countries, this means that
the heretics are not infrequently free prey for the
military and secret services. This creates a situation almost like that of the medieval Inquisition, at
least from the viewpoint of the army. Back then,
however, it was Rome that asked the arm of the state
for assistance in eliminating the heretics. Now "the
sword" acts in its own interest and appreciates the
support of the doctrinal office.

Admittedly, the positive mentioning of different
church dignitaries and staff in the third secret
document indicates that the military and secret
services have their definite church and theological
collaborators.

Cardinal Lopez Trujillo was deliberately appointed,
first as General Secretary and then as President of
the Latin American Bishops' Conference (CELAM) in
1972, in order to get the Latin American churches to

depart from the option for the poor adopted in Medellin. Others followed, like Alberto Methol Ferre,
mentioned in Document III.

Luis Perez Aguirre reveals further interesting facts
in the article mentioned above (Note 30) which we
quote in detail here:

> "Another preferred medium used by the circles
> mentioned is the CELAM database, centralized in
> Bogata as part of a multi-million data processing
> system. It is meant to check on the activities
> of liberation. Apparently the project is far
> more extensive and serves the purpose of collec-
> ting and preserving information on all aspects of
> the events in the Latin American church. Colum-
> bian bishop Dario Castrillon Hoyos, president of
> CELAM, announced last year the completion of the
> first stage of a computer system with satellite
> transmission, which was valued at six million US
> dollars and would connect the bishops conferences
> with Rome and CELAM. The chief equipment of this
> system, a $800,000 computer at CELAM head-
> quarters, has been operating for over three
> years. The system is involved in setting up and
> running two multi-million projects, part of the
> Vatican's new evangelization crusade for Latin
> America: "Evangelizacion 2000" and "Lumen 2000"
> headquartered in Dallas, Texas, the location of
> the "God is Light" charismatic center. The
> international director of the two projects is the
> US Redemptorist priest Tom Forrest. The General
> Secretary of CELAM, Mons. Oscar Rodriguez, stated
> in a recent interview with the magazine "30
> Giorni" of the "Communion y Liberacion" movement,
> that the telecommunications system was trying "to
> combat general disinformation at world level,"
> "disseminated by lay and leftwing agents." He
> denied that the Bogota database had any political
> aims, while Mons. Castrillon admitted that it
> already contained a detailed list of documents,

movements, activities and contacts. "When a theologian travels to a meeting to give a paper or attend a seminar this news is sent to Bogota where it is stored in the computerized system along with information about the agenda and participants."

In this context it is interesting to see the choice of liberation theologians labelled Marxist heretics ("who have excluded themselves from serious theological discussion"). Hugo Assmann, for example, has left the clergy to get married. He and Pablo Richard work at independent theological institutions. So the church is no longer responsible for their welfare. Interestingly, such a well-know name as Leonardo Boff is not on the military hit-list. Through accepting the ordained penance of silence he is under the mantle of the church, with which the military want to cooperate on the terms developed by Rome. It would thus be tactically unwise to attack people with church backing.

2. A further remarkable point about the CIEA documents is that there is no detailed sociological analysis of the different currents in the church. The real social problems to which the Theology of Liberation responds hardly surface again, appearing only in the sense that the "international communist movement" is using these contradictions in its total strategy against the western capitalist system.

Even though the arguments in the documents are largely extremely simplistic, their importance lies precisely in the fact that they are not merely military or militaristic. Completely within the spirit of LIC, the officers participating at the conference have grasped the battle against "communism" not primarily in military terms, but as a political, ideological, economic and secret service-military mission. In an explicit reversal of Gramsci, they attempt to organize and coordinate their struggle for social hegemony.

One can easily understand why the secret documents still react with uncertainty and oversimplification at this point: they are obviously bothered by the Gorbachev phenomenon. Because he does not rely on military confrontation, the military bogeyman is also disappearing. It thus seems plausible to the strategists that Gorbachev has taken over Gramsci's conception that revolution is not to be achieved via armed confrontation but via a re-evaluation of cultural values.[40] They are not particularly careful in their use of terms here. They call the whole phenomenon "Eurocommunism." In fact, Gramsci had a decisive influence on the theoretical and practical attempts of the Italian communist parties in opposition to the Stalinism prevailing at the time, seeking an independent line accepting parliamentary democracy. But this configuration is out of date politically, and it only makes sense to transfer the notion of "Eurocommunism" onto Gorbachev and the whole "international communist movement" if it is stripped of all its historic specificity, and characterized only by the fact that it is no longer concerned for military revolution but for the winning of hearts and minds.

3. International Human Rights
and the Solidarity Movement
in the Face of Disinformation Campaigns

It fits with the simplified and thus dangerous worldview of the military secret services that the CIEA documents want to give the impression that anything they consider highly undesirable is part of a well-laid plot from Moscow (from guerilla movements, drug trafficking and the churches of Latin America to international solidarity and human rights organizations). The enormity of this worldview becomes particularly apparent in the Federal Republic of Germany in that such reputable and hardly revolutionary organizations as the mainline church agencies "Brot fur die Welt" and "Adveniat" are seen as financiers of the "international communist movement." The same fate is suffered by Amnesty International, a human rights organization which takes no account of political blocs. The document serves up a mixture of its own propaganda, military analysis and psychological warfare for serious consumption.

This inclusion of the international solidarity movement and church relief agencies in the category of the communist enemy is highly enlightening for us. When we hear of economic and social injustices and human rights violations in the so-called Third World, we normally see them as individual cases. However, the overall attack, and stressing the struggle in the whole of Latin America as one struggle, make one thing clear; we are confronting a deliberate strategy, not merely tolerated by the western superpower but implemented in full consciousness with the support of the western industrialized countries and the southern governments dependent on them. All churches, groups and movements specifically working for economic and social justice for the mass of the population are to be regarded as enemies. In the interest of defending the present "control and distribution of natural resources" advocated by the capitalist system, are such groups to be combated as expedient by military, secret service and social psychological means.

In this transnational perspective revealed by the Inter-American Armies documents, we can learn to see events in the same light and not in isolation, recognizing their internal connection. Death squads and vigilantes, killing not just local farmers, trade unionists and clergy in Latin America, southern Africa or the Philippines, but also representatives of the international solidarity movement like Pastor Jurg Weis from the Swiss refugee organization in El Salvador[41] - all this is backed by the military, police and judiciary of the "democratic regimes," the southern governments dependent on the USA and the West. This also includes the militarization of education recommended in the Federal Republic of Germany[42] and the USA, and surveillance of peace groups, opponents of nuclear power or even Social Democratic and Green Party members of German Parliament. It is now sufficient to be "indifferent" (not even critical!) regarding the German defense forces in order to be placed under observation (cf. Frankfurter Rundschau, January 18, 1989). Above all, however, the particular aim of the secret services and the military is to influence ideas.

The picture drawn from all this - and space prevents further illustration - is virtually inconceivable for most well-meaning citizens in our countries. We have published these documents from the military secret services and political advisors of the Santa Fe Committee, with reference to similar sources like the Rockefeller Report and the Banzer Plan, in the hope that they will help people in the church and society to come to grips with these hard truths and also to take appropriate action.

We can start with our attitude toward disinformation campaigns, which affect each and every one of us, but particularly churches, unions, schools, universities and media. The secret services see "disinformation" as a method used by the "international communist movement." Certainly it could be argued that all states engage in disinformation or propaganda. No one in the West or the East is in any doubt about that. However, the CIEA documents label as disinformation the reports of human rights organizations, UN-affiliated Non-Governmental Organizations like the

International Commission of Jurists, the churches etc. Since the secret services and military explicitly state that they combat this type of information, it is crystal clear that they themselves are promoting disinformation in the interests of those in power.

The way the authors simply dub as "disinformation" the information given by independent organizations demonstrates their own manipulation of news and facts, which are merely instruments for "psychological operations" to manipulate public opinion. This becomes particularly clear where secret estimations of the situation run counter to governmental information policy. An example of this is the secret service understanding that Costa Rica is a clear ally of the USA and the Sandinista government has the almost total support of the people. Yet the official public line is that Costa Rica is neutral and that the Sandinistas lack support.

Since the conversion to Christianity of the Roman emperor Constantine in the fourth century the western churches and their colonial offshoots have been used to standing at the side of political and, later, economic power. This post-Constantinian church and theology were only questioned with the rediscovery of the bible from the perspective of the poor by the theology of liberation in the countries which European and North American imperialism had exploited and oppressed for 500 years with increasing thoroughness. It was only in this worldwide arousal of the poor that it became clear again that the God of the Bible is in essence against the great power tendencies of the civilizations and intervenes for the weak and marginalized. God frees the slaves from the hand of the oppressors (Exodus 3ff); God wants to form an alternative society among God's people, oriented to the rights of the weak (Ex 21-23); God sends the prophets to preach against the accumulation of wealth and power to demand justice (Jeremiah 22:16); through

Jesus of Nazareth God sets up God's Realm, bringing good news for the poor (Luke 4:16 ff).[43] What appears as the work of evil communism in the secret documents of the western superpower and its allies is, in most of the cases, a matter of working for justice as called for from the perspective of biblical faith — not all forms of struggle for justice are justified, of course. The capitalist "faith" to be defined is the age-old attempt of western colonial and imperialist powers to misuse the God of the Bible as legitimation of their power. Accomplices for that can always be found in the churches. The attempt to suppress the Theology of Liberation by force raises the crucial question for the churches and Christians: Who is God? Is God the justifier of the capital-owners and political powers which want to control natural resources and strategic raw materials and distribute them to their advantage? Or is God the saviour of the poor and thus the bringer of justice for all people and for the threatened earth? This issue has yet to be decided in our countries.

On the other hand, these secret documents have had an immediately positive effect. Churches and solidarity groups often have a feeling of powerlessness when they work for justice and peace. The military and secret services have not proved their effectiveness. So there is still hope.

IV. Questions to Ourselves

What is the point of publishing these secret documents and the story behind them?

First, members of the public interested in democracy can better classify specific international developments through gaining an overall view of the economic, military and social-psychological elements of the strategies that are apparent here. At the same time, they can ask themselves whether they agree with this trend in the so-called free West and how they want to oppose the contours of a violent imperialist strategy.

Secondly, for the same reason we must ask the democratic parties in our western countries whether they intend to support the strategy of total war against the poor as outlined in these documents. They, too, are to be called on to check to what extent our governments, our military, the secret services and our police already have adjusted to the US strategy documented here, and are already participating in it – whether in Latin America, Asia, Africa or the international solidarity and peace movement.

Third, all who feel attracted to neo-conservative and neo-liberal views and values must ask themselves whether they have really thought about the consequences indicated in the documents, and can go along with them.

Fourth, the churches have a unique opportunity, with the aid of these papers to see through, and resist, the attempts made to instrumentalize them. They can also take any attacks of this kind cheerfully. In solidarity with the poor, they can also realize their great importance and responsibility for deligitimizing the West's policy of self-interest. Otherwise they will have to answer for the legitimation they give it. Above all, however, they can vigorously distribute this information and, through challenging the people with responsibility, they can protect individuals, churches and groups suffering for justice's sake in the countries dependent on the West. They have staked their lives – against the forces waging total war against the poor.

Fifth, the human rights and solidarity movements can take heart. Their work counts.

Notes

1.   See: Jochen Hippler, Gefahr der Eskalation – Die Dritte Welt als Objekt der Militarpolitik der Grobmachte, in: Der Uberblick 4/1987, pp.22-25

2.   See e.g.:   US Foreign Policy Objectives and Overseas Military Installations, by the Congressional research Service, prepared for the Committee on Foreign Relations, US Senate, Washington, April 1979.

3.   In the words of President Reagan.

4.   On the history of US Latin American policy in the 19th century see e.g.: Lester D. Langley, Struggle for the American Mediterranean: US-European Rivalry in the Gulf Caribbean, 1776-1904, Athens/GA, 1976; and: Hans Ulrich Wehler, Der Aufstieg des amerikanischen Imperialismus, 1860-1900, Gottingen 1974.

5.   On the history of US Latin America, 1910-1985, Pittsburgh 1985; and selected texts in Jochen Hippler, Menschenrechte and Politik der Starke – USA and Lateinamerika seit 1977, Duisburg 1984, p. 231-235

6.   See: Jochen Hippler, Krieg im Frieden – Amerikanische Strategien dur die Dritte Welt: Counterinsurgency and Low-intensity Warfare, Cologne 1986, p.20 ff.

7.   On LIC in general: Jochen Hippler, Low-Intensity Warfare – Konzeption und Probleme einer US-Strategie fur die Dritte Welt, Working paper No. 1 for the Institute for International Politics (Wupperrtal); and Hippler, Kreig im Frieden, op.cit., p.38ff; Hippler, Low-Intensity Warfare – Key Strategy for the Third World Theatre, in: MERIP Middle East Reports, No. 144, Jan/Feb. 1987, pp.32-38

8.   William J. Olsen, "Airpower in Low-Intensity Conflict in the Middle East," in: Ninth Air University Airpower Symposium, on the Role of Airpower in Low-Intensity Conflict, Maxwell AFB, Alabama, 11-13 March 1985, pp.218, 219, 220

9.   Field Circular "Low-Intensity Conflict," FC 100-20, US Army Command and General Staff College, Fort Leavenworth, Kansas, 30 May 1986

10.   Not all LIC experts would agree with this categorization, though Sam Sarkesian e.g. does not understand explicitly limited conventional operations and terrorism as LIC, although he is clearly out on a limb here. Yet Sarkesian formulates a broad consensus with his statement that "revolution and counter-revolution are the most important categories" of LIC. Sam Sarkesian, Low-Intensity Conflict - Concepts, Principles and Policy Guidelines, in: Air University Review, Vol. 36, No.2., Jan./Feb. 1985, p.5

11.   George Schultz, "Low Intensity Warfare: The Challenge of Ambiguity," in: US Department of State, Current Policy No. 783, January 1986, p.4

12.   Maurice Tugwell/David Charters, "Special Operations and the Threat to the United States in the 1980s," in: Special Operations in US Strategy, publ.by National Defense University and National Strategy Information Center, ed. By Frank R. Barnett, B. Hugh Tovar and Richard H. Schultz, Washington 1983, p.38

13.   John O. Marsh, Keynote Address, in: ibid., p.20

14.   Military Operations - US Army Operational Concept for Low-Intensity Conflict, TRADOC Pam 525-44, Feb. 10, 1986, p.3

15. Caspar Weinberger, in: US Department of Defense, Proceedings of the Low-Intensity Warfare Conference, 14-15 January 1986, Washington, P.2,I

16. Thomas A. Cardwell III, Strategy for Low-Intensity Conflict, in: Ninth Air University Airpower Symposium, on the Role of Airpower in Low-Intensity Conflict, Maxwell AFB, Alabama, 11-13 March 1985, Appendix 2, p.13

17. Jochen Hippler, Krieg im Frieden, op.cit. p.47ff.

18. ibid., p.69ff

19. ibid., and ibid., p.60 ff

20. Jochen Hippler, "Krieg gegen Nicaragua 1981-84," in: Hippler (ed.), Intervention in Mittelamerika und der Karibik - Kokumente und Materialien, Wuppertal 1984 ff. (loose-leaf collection), p.III/1/1-10; and: Hippler: "Krieg gegen Nicaragua - Die Entwicklung der Jahre 1984-85," in: ibid., p III/1.I/1-7

21. On the Reagan doctrine see e.g.: Christopher Layne, "The Real Conservative Agenda," in: Foreign Policy, No. 61, Winter 1985/86, p.73 ff. and: Stephen Rosenfeld, "The Guns of July," in: Foreign Affairs, Spring 1986, p. 698 ff.

22. On Carter's human rights policy as an instrument of US foreign policy: Jochen Hippler, Menschenrechte und Politik der Starke - USA und Lateinamerika seit 1977, Duisburg 1984, p. 45-69

23. Jochen Hippler, Krieg im Frieden, op.cit., pp. 84-97

24. Verbatim protocol by J. Hippler

25. Deryck J. Eller, "Doctrine for Low Intensity Conflict", in: Ninth Air University Airpower Symposium, op.cit., Appendix 2, p.48

26. Committee of Santa Fe (L.F. Bochey, R. Fontaine, D.C. Jordan, G. Sumner, L. Tambs), A New Inter-American Policy for the Eighties, (Council for Inter-American Security) Washington 1980

27. Quotation from: Heinrich Schafer, Befreiung vom Fundamentalismus Entstehung einer neuen Kirchlichen Praxis im Protestantismus Guatemlas, Munster, 1988, p.103

28. Ibid., p. 107 f.

29. "El documento secreto de los golpistas," in: Express (Buenos Aires) Ano 1 - No 4, 15 de mayo 1987, p. 46 ff.

30. See B. Gross, Friendly Fascism, The New Face of Power in America (South End Press) Boston 1982, especially p. 200; U. Duchrow, Weltwirtshaft heute - Ein Feld fur bekennende Kirche?, Munich, 1987, pp. 150ff.

L.P. Aguirre, "Der theologische Arm der Armee," in: BRECHA, Montevideo, Uruguay 30.9.88. One of the chief ideologues in the IRD and American Enterprise Institute is Michael Novak. Cf. Espec.: The Spirit of Democratic Capitalism, New York, 1982 and: Will it Liberate? Questions about Liberation Theology (Paulist Press) New York 1986

31. Committee of Santa Fe (L.F. Bouchey, R. Fontaine, D.C. Jordan, F. Sumner, Jr.) Santa Fe II: A Strategy for Latin America in the Nineties (Council for Inter-American Security) Washington 1989.

32. This term is a variation on the usual "capitalism of national security".

33. The Rockefeller Report on the Americas (Quadrangle Books, Inc.) Chicago 1969

34. Rand Corporation, Latin American Institutional Development: The Changing Catholic Church, ed., L. Einaudi et. al., Washington 1969

35. In: Stimmen der Weltkirche 8, ed. German Bishops' Conference, Bonn 1979

36. Published in: U. Duchrow, op.cit., p. 229 f.

37. Ibid., p. 117 ff.

38. A.M. Ezcurra, The Vatican and the Reagan Adiministration, English edition by New York CIRCUS Publications, Inc., New York, 1986.

39. See below Notes 37 and 40 on CIEA Document 3

40. Antonio Gramsci (1891–1937), Italian philosopher and politician; founder of the Italian Communist Party (1921); imprisoned after its prohibition (1926), released due to ruined health and died in hospital. In detention wrote influential Letters from Prison (pub. posthum. in 1947). His ideas, diverging from Stalinism, have influenced communism and "Eurocommunism" to this day.

41. Cf. Frankfurter Rundschau, 24.1.89

42. Cf. U. Duchrow and R. Eckertz, Die Budeswehr im Schulenterricht. Ein Prozess gegen Indoktrinierung, Baden-Baden 1988

43. Cf. U. Duchrow and G. Liedke, Schalom Der Schopfung Befreiung, den Menschen Gerichtigkeit, den Volkern Freiden, Stuttgart, 1987, pp. 81 ff.

INTELLIGENCE CONFERENCE

OF AMERICAN ARMIES

XVII CONFERENCE

OF AMERICAN ARMIES –CEA–

Buenos Aires – Argentina 1987

DOCUMENT I:
THE DEVELOPMENT
OF THE COMBINED PERCEPTION
(ON SUBVERSION IN THE CONTINENT)
FOR THE INTELLIGENCE CONFERENCE
OF AMERICAN ARMIES -CIEA-

Document I: The Development of the Combined Perception (On Subversion in the Continent) for the Intelligence Conference of American Armies -CIEA

1. Introduction

Reality substantiates that the world finds itself divided into different ideological blocs and political-economic orientations, in a geo-strategic context created in YALTA and POTSDAM, in effect in the nuclear age.

The leading communities must maintain a balance of world leadership based in a global political, economic and military strategy, concurrently and simultaneously adjusted between negotiations and the unleashing of a nuclear holocaust.

The world leadership finds itself emeshed in a real EAST-WEST confrontation, framed in a geographic coordinate, although it is really a confrontation between powers that tend toward the domination and distribution of natural resources and of strategic raw materials.

Transition from the industrial to the post-industrial era requires a reconditioning of NORTH-SOUTH relations, that is between developed communities and the developing communities.

With respect to the frame of reference presented, the overriding need is to resolve the problems of world cooperation, that is, the interdependence to prevent the world from falling under the domination of regressive ideologies, counter to the evolution of humanity.

In this world context, the USSR, the primary object of our study, as the leader of communism, maintains the following goals:

a. Substitution of the democratic capitalist system, by means of subversive-political-terrorist revolutionary war, with the communist system directed toward integrated and worldwide leadership.

b. Channelling of expansionist policies through economic-territorial conquest and ideological control.

c. Soviet persistence in increasing the capacity for nuclear attack and corresponding complete defense capacity in order to counteract the North American counterpart.

d. Simultaneous consolidation and expansion of the military power of the communist bloc (Warsaw Pact) opposed to NATO.

e. Shifting political leadership through the rise of Gorbachov.

At the same time, it is important to point out the presence of communist China which, although still distant from the position of superpower, proposes to obtain Western technology to consolidate its industrial revolution, in an apparent USSR-China doctrinal dissidence.

The International Communist Movement (ICM) through psychological-ideological means takes advantage of the vulnerabilities of the western bloc, the social imbalances, economic dislocations, political failures, splits in leadership and military disagreements.

An important Western vulnerability is its lack of awareness of the global strategy of the Revolutionary War.

It is helpful to caution that, with the military and political individualims of the Western countries, the ICM acts with a sense of political-ideological centralism that poses a real challenge.

2. Analysis of the General Situation

a. The World Situation

1) Marxist-Leninist Communism

The ideological expansionist policy of Marxism-Leninism has as its objective:

a. The substitution of democratic political systems of the Western Bloc with the communist international regime.

b. To participate with the West in world leadership.

c. The physical occupation of strategic areas on land and in space.

The person responsible for this establishment of goals was STALIN and it arose as a result of the combination of MARX's philosophical thought and LENIN's theory of practice.

The leadership of Marxism-Leninism is provided by the Eastern Bloc, by the KREMLIN, strategically oriented toward consolidating its world hegemony and at the same time exporting its political-ideological scheme.

As examples we should cite events such as the encouragement of the South African guerrilla movement in order to control the Cape of Good Hope; destabilizing the governments of the PERSIAN GULF in order to have greater influence in this strategic zone or create a situation similar to that of INDOCHINA; augmenting the guerrilla movement in the PHILIPPINES.

In communist subversion's constant activity, the permanent action of the USSR is significant as the principal promotor of the ICM.

This movement, which has affiliated parties in EUROPE, CENTRAL AMERICA, and SOUTH AMERICA, maintains some differences with other, non-orthodox, communist lines. Nevertheless, it has reached an important level of leadership under the doctrine of pure Marxism-Leninism, the dictatorship of the proletariat, anti-imperialist war, class struggle and the struggle against revisionism.

The "new war" strategy carried out by the ICM implies a particular methodology and new tactics that distinguish it from conventional military conflict.

The operational leadership of communism, more agile, mobile and flexible, implies infinite ideological shading.

Within this new form of war, the Soviets conceived the "war for peace" and make use of the antithesis that "peace is the continuation of war by other means," whose synthesis is the "revolutionary subversive political-terrorist war."

The rise of the charismatic MIKHAIL GORBACHEV leadership to the head of the USSR has strengthened the "zero option" in the context of peaceful relations with the West.

The weakening of NATO with respect to the Warsaw Pact is being pursued.

The distancing of the United States from WESTERN EUROPE through the "zero option" would compromise the security of the continent. At the same time, GORBACHEV seeks to strengthen his position in the internal order in response to the reactions of the more conservative sectors, tending with his policy of "peaceful coexistence" to even out the imbalance between the Eastern Bloc Economic Community (COMECON) and the European Economic Community (EEC).

The USSR is the principal center for the promotion of the current global strategy of Marxism-Leninism. The GORBACHEV administration and the ICM have the following goals:

a) Dominate the principal international commercial routes.

b) Establish a military infrastructure for direct or indirect operations.

c) Limit and weaken their principal adversaries: THE UNITED STATES, WESTERN EUROPE and the PEOPLE'S REPUBLIC OF CHINA.

d) Maintain relations with religious people with progressive tendencies.

The situation is apparently favorable for the ICM, principally due to the skillful actions of GORBACHEV who, by means of glasnost -- openness, transparency -- mobilizes world public opinion in favor of Western disarmament, proposes to lower military spending in order to concentrate on the modernization of the economy, reconstruct the political, economic and military communist system, and meet technological challenges.

2) Maoist Communism

The strategy of international Maoist communism is systematized in the objectives of the International Revolutionary Movement (IRM), founded in LONDON in 1984, in accord with Marxist-Leninist-Maoist ideology that favors armed struggle on a world-wide level by means of the Terrorist International in the countries of the Third World, especially LATIN AMERICA.

The movements identifies as Maoist are not necessarily backed by COMMUNIST CHINA, but rather accept the ideas of MAO TSE TUNG.

In LATIN AMERICA Maoism, beginning in 1980, has been participating in the Peruvian Marxist-Leninist Communist Party, "Sendero Luminoso" (SL), the Shining Path, which began the "Popular and Prolonged War from the Countryside to the City."

The success of the revolution begun by MAO TSE TUNG in CHINA, gave prominence to his strategy, to the extreme that it has come to be considered a paradigm of the theory of Revolutionary War.

MAO, who basically conceived the taking of power by means of prolonged armed struggle with the rural peasants as the principal force of political stratagem, visualized encircling the cities through the action of an army of liberation (whose goal was to wear down what he called the bourgeois army). He also took on some of CLAUSEWITZ's concepts, taken from LENIN, which led him to define war "as a means used by politics when the latter cannot continue to develop as it would wish by normal means."

In this sense, and complementing that statement, MAO said that "war can not be separated, even for an instant, from politics," "from which it follows that the objectives of Revolutionary War are political before they are military."

For Maoist communism, wars are just or unjust not because of the means employed, but because of the objectives intended to be achieved. Within this scheme, the confrontation of subversive groups fulfills a political goal, thus indoctrination is first political in order to pass later to the military aspect.

We are to be warned, then, by the concurrence between the thought of MAO and that of LENIN in the consideration of Revolutionary War as a political and social process before being a military one. This process leads inevitably to the establishment of the new world order.

For Maoist communism, the revolution represents "the new" or "that which will come," in clear contrast to the "former" bourgeois states, representative of the "old." Under such an assumption, the implementation of the strategy without time or space is directed toward gradually wearing down traditional values until the entire society has been transformed. This negative attitude toward "the old" even leads to opportunistic criticism of the basic principles of Marxism-Leninism, calling them "absolute, ingenuous and stupid," and outside the reality of the country at that time.

If it is possible culturally to internationalize this concept of permanent mutability (by means of propaganda), it becomes natural to live in a "youth civilization," in which everything "old" will give way to the "new".

This criterion places CHINA in open opposition to the USSR, with regard to respect for the "wisdom of the elders," personified in its political leadership.

For this ideologue, the principal idea is based on utilization of the democratic game to install Socialism in power. Once this first objective has been achieved, revolutionary communism is to be finally imposed.

Mao's work is aimed principally at intellectuals, professionals and those who control the communication media.

He sustains the idea of the "revolutionary value of the intellectual" to conquer "civil society," necessary for taking power in political society.

This new form could create another stage of international communism, with projections toward an Amero-communism and an Afro-communism, based on:

a) The adoption, in the face of Soviet authoritarianism, of "national paths to Socialism," replacing "international proletariat" with "international solidarity" and strengthening "cultural forces."

b) The defense of pluralist democracy as a period of transition from Capitalism to Socialism, as a substitute for the dictatorship of the proletariat.

All this is a means, not an end.

The intermediate stage of the "dictatorship of the proletariat" is substituted by a multi-party and parliamentary "democratic path"; and once power has been taken in a peaceful and/or violent way, the formal or profound democracy is cast aside.

On the other hand, Eurocommunism is forming direct action groups with terrorist organizations from GERMANY, BELGIUM and PORTUGAL.

At the same time the new communist strategy is projected toward LATIN AMERICA as a form of Amerocommunism, resulting in the combination of the actions of Eurocommunism, the USSR, CUBA and NICARAGUA, in a surreptitious way.

b. The Continental Situation

1) North America

a) In NORTH AMERICA, although it is part of the continent least affected by subversion, the communist intelligence services operate, trying to detect vulnerable points in order to outline an adequate strategy for infiltration.

US economic and political decisions are involved, one way or another, in the intentions of hands of delinquent terrorists to alter the continental order.

Nevertheless, the subversive process in the NORTH AMERICAN countries has been increasing in the last decade and is reflected in the increase of terrorist acts against citizens and property owners, particularly North Americans.

At the same time, there is a notable growing expansion of pacifist and ecological organizations that use violence in defense of their contentions.

Aggression due to drugs, especially affecting the United States, and which is identified with narcoterrorism, is particularly important.

The actions of Marxism—Leninism and Maoism are not present in the United States and CANADA, although communist parties exist.

Eurocommunism, as a Marxist tendency proposing to achieve power through democratic means, is more viable through cultural and intellectual ideological infiltration and, above all, through the questioning of North American western leadership.

At the same time, subversion in the United States includes various forms: propaganda, espionage, and ideological-religious manipulation.

Various subversive groups are active in the US which, while lacking operative capacity for destabilization, carry out terrorist activities that subvert the public order. These include:

(1) Clandestine Resistance.

(2) The Black Panthers.

(3) The Afro-American Liberation Army.

(4) The Black Liberation Army.

(5) Symbionese Liberation Army.

President REAGAN declared that a very sophisticated and successful world-wide disinformation campaign exists, one which has reached the North American media and has successfully infiltrated itself through parliamentary means to influence negatively such themes such as defense, arms control and international politics.

This campaign is promoted by international Marxism.

b) In CANADA, communism encourages separatist movements in the province of QUEBEC, and is infiltrating political and labor union organizations.

Through these methods, espionage activities are included.

c) In MEXICO, communist subversion shows itself sporadically among students and peasants, controlled by the liberal forces.

2) Central America

The conflictive Central American situation of open confrontation among forces (political, diplomatic and military), should be considered a phenomenon with regional characteristics, multiplying effects on the continental and world-wide scale.

Among the notable elements of this phenomenon, which interact as determinant variables of the conflict, the following can be mentioned:

a) The presence, and direct or indirect influence, of the great powers.

b) The position of the greatest worldwide ideological and political currents.

c) The relevant "in situ" activity of organizations with the most diverse characteristics (religious, economic, political-ideological, human rights, etc.)

d) The structurally very grave socioecnomic situation, with no possibilities for becoming primary (mono-crop cultivation).

e) The presence of ethnic groups of different origins, languages and religious beliefs.

f) Psycho-social structures with profound inequalities.

g) The traditional leftist or rightist position of

the principal political parties, notwithstanding the fact that the Central American political spectrum has been complemented with the presence of the Christian

Democrats (center-left), supported by the United States.

h) The activity of political or armed subversion, highly active and opportunist, long in existence, but coordinated since the end of the 1960's.

The principal actors in this conflict are:

a) The CONTADORA Group (CG): MEXICO, PANAMA, COLOMBIA and VENEZUELA, whose mission is that of mediator.

b) The CONTADORA Support Group (CSG): ARGENTINA, BRAZIL, PERU and URUGUAY, whose mission is to support the work of the CG.

c) The HONDURAS, EL SALVADOR and COSTA RICA Coalition, as active opponents of NICARAGUA and declared allies of the United States. In this grouping, the position of the Guatemalan foreign policy of attempted neutrality should be mentioned. Although it rejects the Nicaraguan ideological posture, it supports the CG.

d) CUBA and NICARAGUA, as destabilizing political elements.

e) The armed subversion in EL SALVADOR and GUATEMALA.

These elements in conflict adopt the interests of other countries, of international organizations, of ideological currents that cover the entire spectrum, from the radical left to the radical right, plus the indirect confrontation between the United States and the USSR.

It must be noted that CENTRAL AMERICA has been transformed into one of the most dangerous enclaves of the Theater of Operations of the armed violence resulting from the EAST-WEST confrontation.

The international Soviet communist strategy tries to consolidate its actions in EL SALVADOR, CUBA and NICARAGUA, in order to extend its geo-political dominance toward GUATEMALA, HONDURAS and COSTA RICA, then to take control of the PANAMA Canal, point of convergence of the ATLANTIC and the PACIFIC.

Beginning in 1979, with the triumph of Sandinismo, the option of violence was imposed, coinciding with a strategic change on the part of the USSR which, beginning in 1980 came to consider this area as an immediate political objective.

The Maoism of the 1960's, when Sandinismo was developing its strategy of rural guerrilla warfare, is being replaced by Eurocommunism.

This Takes on Two Forms:

a) political Sandinismo, which brings together diverse Marxist strategies; the traditional left, the intellectual "elite" and a mass of civilians that support it almost completely;

b) a guerrilla force slowly transformed into a regular army that provides both internal and external security.

Faced with the serious EAST-WEST confrontation in the region, diplomatic measures by the United Nations and the OAS with the aid of CONTADORA, are being carried out in order to find a peace via democratic elections in NICARAGUA.

On the other hand, the Central American heads of state, hoping to find a solution to the regional crisis, held a meeting in ESQUIPULAS (GUATEMALA) on August 6 and 7, 1987, signing "Procedures to Establish a Firm and Lasting Peace in CENTRAL AMERICA," that include the following considerations:

a) "The necessity for a dialogue with all disarmed internal political opposition groups and with those who might have accepted a prior amnesty."

b) It is required that the affected governments issue an amnesty decree and, at the same time, that irregular forces of the respective country free all persons under their control.

c) The states of the area that currently suffer the action of irregular or insurgent groups promise to carry out the necessary action to achieve an effective cease-fire and an end to hostilities.

d) The governments from outside the region that openly or covertly provide military, logistical, financial or propagandistic aid, in human resources, arms, munitions or equipment to irregular forces or insurrectional movements must cease that aid as an indispensable element to achieve a stable and lasting peace in the region.

e) The countries are to initiate an authentic democratic, pluralist and participatory process that implies the promotion of social justice, respect for human rights, sovereignty, the territorial integrity of states and the right of all nations to freely determine their economic, political and social model without external interference of any kind.

f) The process must include complete freedom of the press, absolute pluralism for political parties and the elimination of states of siege in those zones where they are currently in effect.

g) The governments of the area request that irregular forces and insurgent groups that function in CENTRAL AMERICA refrain from receiving aid.

h) A Central American Parliament is to be established by electoral means directly charged with finding a solution leading to peace in CENTRAL AMERICA.

An INTERNATIONAL COMMISSION FOR FOLLOW-UP AND VERIFICATION, comprised of the secretaries general or their representatives before the United Nations, the OAS, the Central American foreign ministers and the members of the Contadora Group, are charged with analyzing the process and the agreements, and will present a report to the presidents of the region.

Since this situation favors the interests of the Sandinistas, the Nicaraguan government will comply with the agreement in an attempt to block or strategically limit United States' intervention, and will thereby be able to consolidate their position in the Central American area in order to facilitate communist expansion.

3) South America

a) The countries of this area have demonstrated that they can combat the subversive movement in the military arena.

b) Despite the efforts of the governments to diminish social, cultural and economic differences, these problems persist and are being exploited adequately by the subversion in their campaign of indoctrination of the masses.

c) Differences among the countries of the continent regarding territorial questions are and can be encouraged by the Marxists in order to augment South American disintegration.

d) Since this part of the continent is one of the principal sources of raw material supplies for the United States, head of the Western Bloc, it constitutes one of the most desired objectives of international communism.

e) The ICM objective of Marxist–Leninist infiltration in SOUTH AMERICA is a fact in the Armed Forces, in the church, in workers' and students' organizations. All the social instances are part of the plans of subversion.

f) SOUTH AMERICA is surely the part of the continent most affected by subversion directed from abroad. It is a common denominator in all the countries that struggle against bands of delinquent terrorists supported by training, armaments, and economic aid by international communism from based located outside the region.

g) It is evident, in the region that international terrorism is developing a global strategy for LATIN AMERICA that takes place in SOUTH AMERICA, with the meeting center in WESTERN EUROPE, and which is based on collaboration and interaction of the American and European bands of delinquent terrorists.
   This strategy consists in coordinating programs and carrying out a harmonious and coherent plan with fixed objectives bythe international communist movement for the American continent.

   Currently the SOUTH AMERICAN countries most in turmoil due to terrorist subversion are COLOMBIA and PERU.

   In general, in the rest of the countries of the area, subversion does not appear significant and in some cases with the return of democracy, they are in a stage of reorganization of their structures.

In general, in the South American countries, the subversive situation in the last few years has made itself felt by limited actions through infiltration in political, labor, religious, student and news organizations.

Lately the close connection between the continental and international terrorist movements has been proven, as has the close relationship of the latter to world narcotics traffic, creating narcoterrorism, under the leadership of the ICM.

For political-subversive action, the ICM uses front organizations that operate in LATIN AMERICA for the Communist Party of the USSR, and which encompass all union, student, religious and educational areas.

Marxism-Leninism expresses itself in SOUTH AMERICA through local communist parties.

It can be foreseen that, in the medium term, the majority of these parties could choose the violent or insurrectional course, when they are unable to come to power through electoral means.

Maoism is present in the Shining Path group and since 1980, it has been developing a policy of insurrection based on the predominance of the countryside over the city.

Shining Path has disconnected itself from COMMUNIST CHINA, and has the support of Soviet communism.

Eurocommunism acquired reality in the southern continent after the fall of communism in CHILE, by trying to penetrate political groups and religious sectors with the help of a vast editorial campaign with the appearance of an attractive and non-Leninist left for the masses of potential electorate.

At the same time, the Theology of Liberation (TL) and the humanist parties are part of this scheme.

The subversion in the region is becoming more significant as modernization and democratization advance.

At the same time, subversion has increased due to the connection of the USSR and CUBA in the diplomatic, economic, technological, cultural and informational arenas.

The insurgents of SOUTH AMERICA continue being trained in CUBA and NICARAGUA.

The Cuban intelligence services, backed by the USSR, direct their operations toward consolidating the objectives of Cuban foreign policy.

These objectives consist in sustaining the Sandinista government in NICARAGUA.

On the other hand, the Cuban intelligence services threaten the operational security of the United States forces on the continent.

In synthesis, the Soviet-Cuban-Nicaraguan triangle is developing maximum capacity for the exporting of insurgencies throughout LATIN AMERICA.

3. Specific Situations of the Countries

a. ARGENTINA

The proximity of national, provincial and municipal elections on September 6, 1987 has meant an increase in activism of the surface organizations of the delinquent terrorist bands (DTB).

Montoneros–Revolutionary Peronism (PR), despite some important successes in terms of its insertion within the Partido Justicialista (PJ), appears to have reached its possible limit within this operation, thus a significant lack of satisfaction can be observed among its leaders and members. The membership is largely emigrating toward the ranks of so-called "combative Peronism," which makes up the Party of the Shirtless For Victory (PDPV) and the Peronist Movement 26 of July (MP–26). Both political currents are allied with the Communist Party (PC), within the Broad Liberation Front (FRAL), and are of an insurrectional character.

The leaders of the Montoneros–PR have gone to CUBA in the last few weeks to achieve release of funds that the DTB has deposited in HAVANA, along with permission for greater participation within the revolutionary process in ARGENTINA and in the entire Southern Continent.

The trade union arm of this sector of Montoneros has serious difficulties in recruiting followers, which has frustrated one of its principal objectives for 1987. With respect to the Barrial Front, another area in which the group sought to recover spaces according to its objectives, it was the "combative" sector which achieved greater success, principally in GREATER BUENOS AIRES, the INDUSTRIAL CORRIDOR OF LA PLATA (PBA)-VILLA CONSTITUTION (SANTA FE) and CORDOBA.

For both political lines of the Montoneros, action against the Armed Forces continues to be the main objective, including the campaign of defamation with respect to supposed violations of human rights, which attempts to create confusion ABOUT certain high officials (particularly of the Army), to cause doubt and a loss of prestige. With respect to armed activity, the "combatives" are the most advanced in this regard, linked to the military wing of the PC, as well as to the dissident faction of the Workers' Revolutionary Party-People's Revolutionary Army (PRT-ERP), which is reorganizing its military front.

Particularly in the PRT-ERP, the struggle between the two existing internal political lines has been especially interesting during the pre-electoral period. The political current that places priority on political action came out of the Seventh Congress of the PRT formally strengthened and achieved an impressive propagandistic display through its front organizations: the Popular Anti-Imperialist Democratic Movement (MODEPA), the All For the Homeland Movement (MTP), the Popular Democratic Left (IDEPO)-- that function at the national level—and others that function in the provinces and municipalities under their own names. Nevertheless, the objective of this activity turned out to be clearly limited to the diffusion of subversive slogans and the recruitment of followers for their armed wing.

This methodology of the MODEPA political line is not shared by the NICARAGUA political line, whose leadership believes that the growing line of the political insurrection process is changing course, and therefore it is reorganizing the ERP and developing an intense propaganda campaign in favor of maximalist positions and immediate objectives.

Likewise, elements of this political line maintain positions in the legalized structures of the group, which makes their interaction more efficient and facilitates the involvement of both factions in violence, in case the situation erupts.

The Multi-sectorial Bureau of Permanent Mobilization and the Committees for the Defense of Democracy, which exist on various levels, fulfil--like the FRAL on the political-electoral level--the function of reference points for coordination between the DTBs, and between them and the rest of the subversive spectrum, with political, propagandistic and cultural goals at the moment.

One of the other principal subversive fronts are the Marxist Political Organizations (MPO), that correspond to the three ideological lines of world Marxism-Leninism: the Soviet, the Trotskyist and the Maoist. The Communist Party (PC) corresponds to the first, while the Socialist Movement (MAS), the Workers' Party (PO) and the Posadista Revolutionary Workers' Party (PORP) correspond to the second. The Revolutionary Communist Party (PCR), the People and Work Party (PTP) (the legal arm of the PCR), and the Liberation Party (PL) belong, on the other hand, to the Maoist line.

In order of importance, the PC, the MAS and the PO are the most active of all, although the growth of the PTP during 1986 and 1987 should not be ignored. These four organizations are the only ones that have achieved the status of a political party at the national level. The PC and the PORP are very small groups, although, in the case of the former, potentially dangerous since it proposes armed struggle as the methodology for achieving power.

While it is true that, after the military events of Holy Week in 1987, there have been, in general, a turn toward extremist positions among the MPOs and, in some cases, such as that of the PC, the MAS and the PO, toward adopting plans to counter similar situations through armed struggle and the AIM. In this regard, it must be kept in mind that the PC has been working on organizing and extending its military wing since 1974, and that the MAS and the PO have been moving toward AIM because of its own ideological conviction.

More important than the creation of plans there already have been concrete events, in the sense of developing organizations capable of armed struggle. The military training provided by NICARAGUA for the members of the various "Coffee Brigades" organized by the Communist Youth Federation (FJC) should be mentioned, the last of which, called ARGENTINE FALKLANDS, was composed of members from different parties. At the same time, the PC has distributed arms among its Self-Defense Groups (GA), while the MAS is in the process of arming itself, operating like its common criminal suppliers. On the other hand, members of the PC, the MAS and the PO have gone into hiding in various places of the country.

Parallel with these activities, the MPOs with electoral standing have carried out intense political activity with their sites on the September 6, 1987 provincial, municipal and legislative elections. In this way the PC has created, together with other Left parties and groups, the Broad Liberation Front (FRAL), while the MAS and the PO came together with their lists of candidates. The PTP leaned, on the other hand, toward supporting the Peronist candidates for provincial seats, urging their affiliates to cut ballots.

The pre-electoral polls carried out until the present, as well as the results of the anticipated provincial elections, carried out in SAN JUAN Province, indicate that the FRAL maintains the historical electoral support of the PC (close to one percent of the electorate), while the MAS shows notable growth in the province of BUENOS AIRES (the country's most important electoral district).

The third important front involves the Solidarity Organizations (SO). Events generated by them, since the mid-1986 to the present, must be understood within the framework of their decreasing influence over the PO, which results in displacement of their center of gravity toward a campaign to enable them to reverse their loss of prestige and decreased capacity of mobilization.

To that effect, the chosen methodology largely determined their activities, and attacks against the Armed Forces and/or Security Forces were carried out by means of denunciations (regarding commission of various crimes), refutation (of promotions, speeches, etc.), insults (offenses, provocations, etc.), propaganda (accusations against people supposedly responsible for human rights violations, pamphleteering, marches, etc.).

At the same time, actions of harassment were carried out against national government: regarding its human rights policy (the "two demons" theory), so-called "political repression" (cases of common delinquency that are exploited politically) and by the legislation "favorable" to the Armed Forces (the ratification of "punto final" and "obediencia debida" laws).

For its part, the Judicial Branch was accused of: "lack of independence" with respect to the national government, (charges against the Supreme Court of Justice, against lower judges that decide against their positions, etc.).

The Legislative Branch also was criticized: for its complicity with the national government, by ratifying laws around the issue, which protect members of the Armed Forces from criminal charges; for delay in dealing with the issue of the so-called "political prisoners"; for failing to create bicameral commissions to investigate the issue of human rights; and for agreeing to the military's conditions, presumably connected to the struggle against terrorism.

Their Psychological Action toward the rest of the world made concrete in the exaltation of American Marxist regimes.

On the other hand, their political activity is centered on moving closer to the MPOs, through agreements that are rarely made public but which are made clear by the participation of the MPOs in the acts of the SOs or by internal confrontations which—like the one involving the Human Rights Association—are carried out as public acts of political support, in this case in favor of the FRAL.

b. BOLIVIA

BOLIVIA has constituted a permanent objective of conquest for international subversion, and for that reason various subversive processes have occurred, that run from social agitation to armed struggle.

The different Marxist ideological lines are present in the current subversive activity affecting the country; each of them have succeeded in establishing their presence in various political, trade union and workers' organizations that are actively participating in national events.

During recent times, the country's political, economic and social situation has created and left among the masses of the population a state of disorientation, instability, uncertainty and resistance against almost all forms of authority and governmental administration.

The national economic reorganization has demanded of the government the adoption of drastic measures, which have affected the socio-economic structure while altering the position of leadership that some sectors exercised, so that some, like the mining sector, now seem lowered to an irrelevant position within the social political context.

The most important activities carried out by subversion are the following:

1) Massive psychological action over the population through the media.

2) Alteration and upsetting of the ethical values and morals of the people, their authorities and institutions.

3) Attempt to reduce the prestige and break the unity of the Armed Forces at its various levels of command.

4) Continuous indoctrination and ideological consciousness raising among the mining, student, manufacturing, teacher and peasant sectors.

5) Infiltration and taking over leadership and bases of the various social, political, cultural, religious, trade union, etc. organizations, throughout the Republic.

6) Clandestine organization of subversion's "Political Military Organization."

7) Organization and establishment of support bases for international subversion.

Within the continental context, international subversion seeks to convert Bolivian territory into a base for its operations abroad, particularly in neighboring countries. To this end, clandestine front organizations of all kinds have been developed, some dedicated to propaganda, indoctrination and training of the population, and to reducing the prestige of the authorities and legal institutions of

the State; others are dedicated to direct insurrectional action through sabotage, terrorism,
strikes, work stoppages, occupations of buildings,
etc., which are all part of subversive activity.

To carry out these types of activities, elements
belonging to the principal subversive organizations
of the continent were installed in the country, such
as: the Manuel Rodriguez Patriotic Front (FPMR) of
Chile, the Shining Path Peruvian Communist Party
(PCP-SL) of PERU, the People's Revolutionary Army
(ERP) of ARGENTINA, which in collaboration with
activities of the Bolivian Communist Party (PCB) and
with diplomatic delegations accredited in the
country, place the stability and security of the
country at risk.

The dynamism that the subversive process has
acquired recently can be seen in permanent social
upheaval based on "contempt" for authority, where the
educational sectors, miners, students and the
Bolivian Workers' Central (COB), are the vanguard of
the social failure at the national level.

While it is true that the social factor was the
epicenter of subversive action through leadership of
the various sectors, the political factor, and within
it the fractions, fronts, leftist and ultra-leftist
parties, carried out intense activity, characterized
by a permanent opposition and obstruction of governmental administration, and support for, and taking
advantage of, in any conflict that is generated in
the social sphere.

The ultra-leftist fractions have sought to
create political fronts that would permit them to
have a greater representation within the workers
organizations, for which some of them have created
the Axis of Patriotic Convergence (ECP) as the
largest political-subversive organization around

which all structures with "contempt for authority" as their slogan have been organized.

The aim of this axis is the rejection of the socio-economic policies of the government, and the creation of a leftist front to bring together other anti-government revolutionary fractions under their leadership. Its goal is to take power through an armed insurrection of the people.

The current center of activity is the infiltration and takeover of the key organization of Bolivian trade unionism, the COB.

The various fractions of the Revolutionary Workers' Party (POR) constitute the foundation of activism and mass work in the current subversive situation. Each one of them (POR-COMBATE, POR-DEPIE, POR-LORA, POR-VANGUARDIA COMUNISTA, and POR-UNIFICADO) in their own way have succeeded in reaching important positions in the teachers', students' and peasants' unions, among workers, which are the sectors where their activity is centered.

Completing the picture of the leftist organizations, we should point out that there are those which adopt a critical position with respect to the government's policies within the democratic scheme. There are other organizations along the lines of European Social Democracy, Castroism, Maoism and anarcosyndicalism.

Within this framework, the FREE BOLIVIA Movement (MBL) appears to be the most active ultra-leftist fraction and clandestinely organizes its members for armed struggle.

c. BRAZIL

Subversive activity currently is being carried out through political-ideological action, taking advantage of the pluralist constitutional system of the country.

It is characterized by intense action that tends to spread Marxist ideology into all spheres of national life, thus creating a favorable climate for the Brazilian Communist Movement (MBC).

This subversive activity is fundamentally oriented toward achieving an effective infiltration in all spheres, particularly penetration of the political parties, especially in the larger parties such as the Workers' Party (PT), the Democratic Brazilian Movement Party (PMBD) and the Democratic Workers' Party (PDT); the educational sphere; the union movement; the MCS, the church, and even the federal, state and municipal administrations, the Legislative Branch and, consequently, in the National Constituent Assembly.

Activity similar to that of the Brazilian workers' centrals is carried out, such as the General Confederation of Workers (CGT)--of moderate tendencies--and in the Unified Workers' Central (CUT), of a more radical tendency.

With respect to "progressive sector pastoral work" of the Catholic Church, its ever-increasing participation in issues of the worldly order is notable, working with the poorer sectors in the country.

At the same time, a very critical attitude toward government authorities and the Armed Forces can be observed. Publications are supported that give information about the anti-subversive struggle, carried out during the recent military government.

d. COLOMBIA

Upon analyzing the current behavior of the subversion in COLOMBIA, it is necessary to point out that armed subversive organizations have exploited the process of "democratic opening" initiated in Dr. BELISARIO BETANCUR CUARTAS's administration. At the same time, taking advantage of such circumstances the DTBs grew, strengthened themselves and provided themselves with logistical means for carrying out political-subversive work of broad national and international scope.

The Armed Revolutionary Forces of COLOMBIA (FARC) also operate politically, and in this sense all their elements support and give wide backing to the political work of the "Patriotic Union" (UP), since it constitutes a positive strategy for the political-armed plans of the insurgents, acquiring greater cohesion and capacity to confront the government and the Armed Forces.

The perspectives of "unity of action" between the FARC and the National Guerrilla Central (CNG) are relative, although the Popular Liberation Army (EPL), the organization with the greatest differences with the pro-Soviet group, has entered into clear agreements, thus overcoming what had appeared to be irreconcilable differences with the extremist grouping. Nevertheless, the process is considered slow and filled with obstacles, such as the issue of external dependency and the desire of the FARC to impose themselves as vanguard.

The proposals that FARC has been advancing and making known to the government, to public opinion, and to the other DTBs, are nothing more than an insurgent strategy to prolong the process by maintaining a permanent position for advancing and deepening their political space, while seeking points of convergence with the other insurgent groups in order to employ greater armed actions in confrontation with the government.

For its part, the National Liberation Army (ELN) proposes to launch activities in favor of the "national popular assembly" as well as "unity of action" activities as part of the initiatives to confront the plans of the military forces and to support popular mobilization.

As an ideological basis, the ELN struggles to take power through armed action without committing itself to electoral objectives, programs or processes that would mean being submitted to traditional systems of popular voting.

This DTB is involved in trying to break the national economy, using anarchist terrorism among basic sectors (in energy and mining), which creates social upheaval and discourages international investment.

The Popular Liberation Army (EPL), political movement in charge of managing Marxist goals in relation to the election of mayors, launched a "Popular Front" project, a regional and national proselytizing campaign to collect 10,000 signatures as a base of support before the State Electoral Council in order to achieve their legalization , which in fact happened on August 11, 1987.

This initiative had the goal of making the EPL a legal entity, of seeking "unity of action" with other DTBs, (especially the FARC), in both the political and armed spheres.

Nevertheless, it is clear that the ideological radicalism of the EPL will cause friction within the CNG which will in some way affect the degree of unity that is being attempted.

The April 19 Movement (M-19) has fixed as its specific work (with respect to its political goals) the creation of a "democratic plan of political, economic and social emergency," a result of agreements with unions, peasants, indigenous group, the small and medium industry and political organizations.

The M-19 political proposal would appear to be limited in certain ways by social plans that the government is introducing the "political opening" which permitted the approval of the election of mayors and consequent strengthening of the traditional parties.

Currently, M-19, fulfilling its proposals and following communist direction, is diverging a little from its trajectory and its extremist character, in order to make possible a dialogue and a subsequent process of "unity of action" around its only objective, the "taking of power" or the "generalized insurrection."

e. CHILE

Historically, it is possible to observe that, since the second half of this century, Marxism-Leninism has passed through three clearly defined stages.

The first of began in the '60s, when the Movement of the Revolutionary Left (MIR) appeared as the only expression of insurrection in LATIN AMERICA. During this period, the Chilean Communist Party was in favor of the electoral and peaceful path, in open disagreement with the MIR.

The second stage began with the government of SALVADOR ALLENDE, a movement in which the Communist

Party maintained its rejection of violence. The socialist movement leaned toward insurrection, expressed through the thesis of the creation of a popular power, which was nothing more than the creation of a parallel to institutional power, that would prevent power being handed at the time designated by the Constitution.

The third stage began in 1980. While it is true that, in 1973, the fall of the ALLENDE government took place, this did not lead to changes in the attitude of the Communist Party. Only recently, in 1981, did it experience a turnaround and decide to embard upon the insurrectional path, permitting its organization to enter the Manuel Rodriguez Patriotic Front (FPMR). This change was caused by two factors, the first an internal one, as a reaction to the military government institutionalized through the Constitution, which it sought to overthrow. The other factor was an external one, responding to Soviet guidance that directed local communist parties toward radicalization and violent struggle.

The Marxist-Leninist opposition in CHILE is currently acting in an analogous form to that of Sandinismo in NICARAGUA, for the following reasons:

1) It seeks to consolidate a mass front of a rupturing or agitational type, for which it relies on the National Workers' Command (CUT), led by a communist.

2) It has a political front, the Popular Democratic Movement (MDP), which allows it to dialogue and be connected with the centrist and moderate left forces.

3) It has an armed structure, represented by the FPMR, the MIR and other smaller groups.

From the political point of view, since the fall of ALLENDE, a political current has been developing within a Gramsian model, as a means of analyzing the reasons for that occurrence.

In terms of critical political analysis, it is inferred that the principal causes were: trying to copy the Soviet scheme in a mechanistic way, and the incapacity to elaborate a specific theory suitable for Chilean socialism, adapted to the socio-cultural reality of the country.

This political current, that comes from very intellectual levels, is gaining acceptance among the left, while slowly permeating the parties of that tendency.

Currently, this tendency is represented in two political parties, the Movement of Popular Unity Action (MAPU) and the NUNEZ Socialist Party (PSN). The latter has the most important leftist intellectuals among its ranks and is elaborating a policy of convincing and moving closer to the parties of the center.

In the near future, these parties could place themselves in the framework established in the process toward democracy. Their action is centered in the cultural field, in the arts and in the proposal of a non-violent solution. This last element is presented as an attractive alternative for the citizenry in general.

In the overtly subversive-terrorist realm, orthodox Marxism-Leninism is active in insisting on the insurrectional path, and activities are directed toward provoking a political crisis in 1989.

In this sense, it is important to note that both the FPMR and the MIR will continue making significant efforts toward disturbing the public order, so that they may remain viable and thus justify the aid that they receive from abroad, while they recreate the logistical and military structures which permit them to carry out some type of action of national importance over the medium term, in pursuit of their tireless objective to do everything possible to obstruct the normal development of the process toward full democracy set in motion by the Chilean government.

f. ECUADOR

In this country, the subversive action of the ALFARO VIVE CARAJO (AVC) or the MONTERA ALFARISTA (MA) DTBs is significant.

Its activities began toward the end of 1984 and it has tried to obtain the support of the Ecuadoran people for their struggle, which undermines the social peace of the country.

The ideological principles on which this organization is based are: unity for democracy, for the Nation, and for Justice, economic democracy and economic independence, social justice, national sovereignty, democracy and the great Latin American homeland.

The ALC delinquent terrorist band has a political-military structure which is conspiratorial, selective, compartmentalized, clandestine, vertical and centralized. It defines itself as a democratic, nationalist, anti-imperialist and internationalist organization.

At the beginning of 1986, this organization suffered a division due to differences within the ruling leadership, at which time the MONTONERA FREE HOMELAND (MPL) was created.

The psychological activities and propaganda of these groups is limited, but not totally without effect, which means that subversion continues to be a latent threat.

g. EL SALVADOR

Subversive action in EL SALVADOR is not recent. Nevertheless, the state of generalized violence that we are currently experiencing began in 1979, and reached significant proportions with the beginning of what, in January 1981, was called the "general offensive."

Since then, communism has chosen difference channels (armed struggle, united front, dialogue). In order to take power, all sectors of the population which they have manipulated are taken advantage of at various times.

In the armed struggle, the Farabundo Marti Front for National Liberation (FMLN) has advanced its war of attrition and preparation of revolutionary forces and the general offensive for taking of political power. This implies logistical provisioning on a large scale, development of an offensive capacity of regular units (Popular Army) and acquiring a secure rearguard.

In the war of attrition, three types of forces are utilized: the guerrillas in the zones, the popular militia and the popular army. The current phase supposes the generalization of the conflict throughout the country and logistical provisioning.

The general offensive implies guaranteeing a solid rear guard, lines of external provisioning for the combat fronts, an annihilation offensive against strategic military units of the Salvadoran Armed Forces (FAES), and the dispute for national territory.

The objectives of subversion in the armed struggle have consisted in inhibiting the movement of the FAES and obliging them to maintain a fixed position or go into their barracks, in order to later disperse them, weaken them, while at the same time striking against their rearguard.

Within this framework, the war takes place in all areas, not only the military, but in all economic, psychological and political spheres, within the concept of low intensity conflict.

The United Front strategy is the accumulation of forces of all the opposition sectors into a political army, which, by means of preconceived platforms, organizes, mobilizes and agitates until the masses can be led to insurrection.

In a communist revolutionary process, the step prior to the offensive for taking of power is mass insurrection. This insurrection must be based on objective and subjective causes, that communism creates through prolonged popular war.

To guarantee the taking of power, the communist revolutionary process is designed in a closed, cyclical way. In this way, time is eliminated as a factor, which makes it possible to begin or end a cycle as desired, while correcting the errors of past cycles.

Since the beginning of the so-called general offensive, the FMLN has gone through different cycles, outstanding among which is the so-called "Preparatory Phase for the Strategic Counteroffensive." The following are its stages, in chronological order:

1) Mobilization of the masses in the months of April, May and June.

2) Recruitment and Political Radicalization in July, August and September.

3) General Strike, systematic urban terrorism and insurrection in October, November and December.

Once this process is completed, the FMLN is in a position to close this cycle with another attempt to take power.

The communist scheme is carried out at a time when the crisis is deepened by military conflict which interferes in the socio-economic and political conditions of the great majority of Salvadorans, worsening health, education, employment, housing and security problems.

The role of the FAES turns out to be complex, in that it is circumscribed within the defense of the democratic process and the guarantee of respect for human rights. This has been an influence for progressive correction of the apparent causes of the conflict in the economic, social and political spheres.

h. UNITED STATES

Subversion in the UNITED STATES acquires distinct forms of expression.

Specifically in United States territory, armed subversion is insignificant. Nevertheless, the North American military bases placed at strategic points are the object of multiple terrorist attemptson the part of different international DTBs.

Public, political, and diplomatic functionaries and executives of American companies, and even ordinary citizens, which for different reasons find themselves spread out over the five continents, are also the victims of attacks and acts of violence.

Subversive action the USSR becomes truly important in the areas of ideological penetration, the collection of classified and confidential information, the transfer of advanced technology, the application of the "active measures," the use of secret agents and the manipulation of the communications media.

The USSR continually tries to penetrate the upper echelons of the North American government. At the same time, it tries to establish new consulates, in order to improve technological intelligence and in that way consolidate an "official network" of agents in the United States.

While it is true that the official Soviet presence has been considerably reduced in 1986, due to clear presidential directives, this did not in any way eliminate the threat posed by espionage and leaking of secret information about government and Defense Department plans.

It is important to point out that commercial activities (clearly expanding) serve as a cover to obtain information in areas that otherwise would be prohibited to Soviet diplomats and functionaries.

From another point of view, propaganda plays an important role in USSR strategy, with regard to the manipulation of international public opinion against the United States.

To that effect, the USSR is implementing what are known as "active measures," which include disinformation, espionage, sabotage, psychological action campaigns, the use of direct and indirect agents, influential groups, etc.

It is impossible to mention here the numerous and prolific campaigns of disinformation, espionage and penetration which for years have jeopardized the highest echelons of North American security.

To this end, the USSR has launched and promoted the activity of various front organizations such as the World Peace Council, with the objective of stimulating disarmament and blaming the United States for the current arms race and the ominous consequences of the use of nuclear weapons with purely bellicose objectives.

Finally, the USSR seeks to compromise the various levels of national security through the use of third countries, and in this regard the Warsaw Pact countries play a fundamental role.

i. GUATEMALA

Subversive groups currently engage in efforts to take power using all means at their command, even taking advantage of acts of violence to terrorize the population.

They carry on work in their respective areas to achieve their various objectives. In the political realm, they seek the isolation of, and conflict between, the Government and the Army. In the ideological sphere, they attempt to destroy the image of the Army and penetrate the private sector, the Church, the State organizations, pressure groups and the media.

Internally, the Guatemalan DTBs are attempting to continue to organize political-military cells clandestinely, both in the urban and rural sectors and take advantage of the organization of the Civil Defense Committees.

The Guerrilla Army of the Poor (EGP) is carrying out an intense propaganda campaign, both at the national and international levels, exploiting the situation of refugees and the displaced in order to discredit the Army and the Government. They are currently involved in winning and recruiting the peasant population through the Committee of Peasant Unity (CUC).

The Organization of the People in Arms (ORPA) is developing in what constitutes the most productive area of the country. From there, it organizes and leads the mass organizations of the Altiplano, the coast and the city in order to obtain popular support.

In the military sphere, they have not presented a defined front.

The Armed Rebel Forces (FAR) operate throughout various northern, southern, central and eastern regions of the country.

They effect the concentration and dispersion of their forces to carry out their armed actions. They provoke the Army and oblige it to pass through areas where ambushes, assaults, etc., have been prepared in advance. They seek to spread terror, threatening the lives of those who collaborate with the Army.

The Guatemalan Work Party (PGT) functions particularly in the population centers of international political influence. This party is trying, without success, to penetrate the various social groups. It seeks to become the principal labor element of the insurgent movement, with the intention of achieving the radicalization of the masses.

The Guatemalan National Revolutionary Unity (URNG) seeks to support all armed actions of the EGP, ORPA, the FAR including them in all national and international reports, and attributing them to actions by the URNG.

They rely for this on the support of foreign journalists, as in the particular case of the International Center for Information Reports on Guatemala (CERIGUA).

j. HONDURAS

The majority of the DTBs were practically annihilated between 1983 and 1984. Among them was the Morazanista Front for National Liberation (FMLN), the "Lorenzo Zelaya" Revolutionary Front, the Central American Workers Party (PTC) and the People's Popular Army (ERP).

Toward the end of 1986, the Honduran Army deactivated the solidarity organization "Cinchoneros" Popular Liberation Front (FLP-Cinchoneros), which operated in the ATLANTIDA and COLON departments.

In this context the activity of the Innovation and Unity Party (PINU), a legal party of the extreme left, and which posseses important economic resources, deserves mention. This party operates through permanent confrontation among the political authorities, the Armed Force, students and union members.

Student and labor organizations are fully infiltrated, and its elements are located in important posts and places.

The PINU rejects the presence of the United States in HONDURAS. It accepts the NICARAGUAN Marxist orientation as a reality, and proposes a political understanding between the two countries.

Recently, in the confrontation between Honduran and Nicaraguan soldiers, the center of gravity exploded against the government through the pressure to remove the anti-Sandinistas from Honduran territory. "Commander J" of the Armed Forces was accused of "not fulfilling his constitutional function, and offering himself as mediator in the delivering of aid to the NICARAGUAN insurgents."

PINU holds fourth political place in the country, after the Liberal Party (PL), the National Party (PN) and the Christian Democratic Party (CD); but it has an efficient organization and Commitments with organizations of countries in the communist orbit are not known.

In general, it is probable that the radicalized elements of the country will try to re-initiate armed activities. It is probable that they will be encouraging the creation of adequate circumstances to justify activities using those means.

In this regard, the pressures exercised by PINU and by the government's state of indecision with respect to the anti-Sandinistas and the ideological-political controversies with their neighbors, are favorable to the above.

k. PANAMA

The Party of the Panamanian Communists (the People's Party), linked to MOSCOW, through CUBA, tries to radicalize the Marxist-Leninist actions in the country.

It first functioned clandestinely and, with the democratic opening, registered in 1981 as a political party, although its legality was annulled in 1984 for not having obtained the necessary votes, in accordance with the law.

Errors in leadership of the party have broken it into small ultra-left groups which, and their activities are limited to maintaining a critical and opposing line to the government, as well as provoking sporadic street disturbances.

Communism's intent is centered on trying to get control over the leadership of the National Workers Central of PANAMA and over the student sectors.

The action of the Liberal Forces has succeeded in inhibiting, in large measure, the Marxist—Leninist objectives of institutional infiltrating and winning over the masses.

Leftist divisions and the anti-communist and religious nature of the people reduce to a minimum the possibilities for ideological penetration and/or changing the way of life.

I. PARAGUAY

Since 1963, all armed subversive attempts that were organized and prepared from neighboring countries by the International Communist Movement with the support of those leftist sectors of political parties, and which, allied with the Paraguayan Communist Party (PCP), led the country into civil war in 1947, have been aborted.

While it is true that no expressions of violence have been observed, the existence of opposition groups which express themselves through political means can be shown.

The action of the Authentic Radical Liberal Party (PLRA) is notable in that it is made up of a group of left-leaning leaders from the Radical Liberal Party (PLR), who reject the leadership of the RLP and the Liberal Party (PL), as well as the Central Electoral Board (JEC), and who question the Electoral Law currently in effect in PARAGUAY. The party includes a group of youth who are experts in Capital, as well as some sympathizers in the interior.

The Popular Colorado Movement (MOPOCO) and the National Republican Association in Exile and Resistance (CANR/E y R) are made up of groups of ex-Colorado leftist leaders who, until some years ago, had their members in neighboring countries, from whence they carried out subversive activities, in alliance with the PCP and delinquent terrorist groups, whose actions are permitted today in PARAGUAY.

The Ethical and Doctrinaire Movement of the Colorado Party, a splinter group of some leaders of the National Republican Association (ANR) who question the former and current leadership of the party, complete the spectrum of opposition to the government.

m. PERU

Over a period of seven years of continuing and permanent armed struggle, Peruvian subversion has demonstrated a capacity to adapt its strategy to the political-military reality it confronts.

The actions carried out at the national level and achievements in the areas of organization, action, agitation-propaganda and intelligence allow us to evaluate that the subversive process in PERU is framed within what, in the Insurrectional Period, could be called the "Generalization of Violence"

Subversive actions have been carried out in almost all the country's provinces. We observe:

1) The establishment of a principal axis that involves the Andean region and which runs from North to South.

2) The creation of secondary or sub-axes in the rural zones in the coastal provinces.

3) The intensification of subversive actions in urban zones, as a complement to rural activity.

The activities carried out by Sendero Luminoso (SL) (the Shining Path) and the TUPAC AMARU Revolutionary Movement (MRTA) are significant.

The Shining Path's strategy is designed to gain political presence in order to influence public opposition both nationally and internationally, accelerate the pace imposed by the leadership for achieving objectives, and maintain the initiative, neutralizing or surpassing the success of counterinsurgency activities by the government.

Until now the Shining Path's activities have been characterized by:

1) A broad geographic sphere of influence (central forest sector, southern sector and the northern provinces).

2) An intense political activity among the remote Andean communities, with the aim of preparing bases of revolutionary support.

3) Increase of propaganda and agitation activities and terrorism, with the goal of winning the support of the largest number of people possible by using this psychological weapon.

4) Broad preparation and training of members, in terms of the number of actions carried out, with the view toward increasing the ranks of the Popular Guerrilla Army.

The MRTA, which is a more open movement that the Shining Path, has a less radical program. For this reason it has the possibility of growing as an organization and incorporating other leftist groups that still remain in the non-violent path.

Currently, the MRTA is in the pre-revolutionary or armed propaganda stage. In this context the MRTA seeks to:

1) have influence and presence in the urban zones of some provinces;

2) unite with a fraction of the Movement of the Revolutionary Left. This would increase its power and organization, and improve its operative capacity, permitting a gain of more political ground;

3) recruit an important sector of university students, workers and professionals with armed propagand;

4) reate expectations of social changes in a sector of the population.

In the last few months the subversive phenomenon at the national level has shown a decrease in those zones where large-scale actions against the Liberal Forces were carried out.

A change can be observed in the attitude of subversion, which is reflected in the replacement of armed actions for psychological and propaganda activities.

The Solidarity Organizations have come to understand that, if they can mobilize, agitate and concentrate without combat, it is entirely inconvenient to provoke unnecessary government repression.

Supporting this change in attitude, some written communications media (the dailies MARCA, CAMBIO and LA VOZ) are carrying out a campaign designed to spread information on subversive actions at the national and international level, by which conscious-

ness raising of the masses is promoted and a general state of tension and insecurity is created.

It can be observed that the subversion takes advantage of the autonomy of the university for carrying out acts of agitation with the direct or indirect participation of students and university authorities. The open presence of the Shining Path has been noted in these acts, which creates a precedent for similar future actions.

The fact that both the Shining Path and the MRTA have modified their strategies does not mean in any way that they have abandoned their methods or the nature of the armed struggle, but rather that they seek opportune moments to re-initiate their actions according to their plans at each moment.

In this context, it is estimated that the Shining Path will continue to consolidate and expand its "Support Bases" in its principal theater of operations (rural zone) in the immediate future. In its secondary theater of operations or axis (urban zone) it will continue its actions of dynamiting and fire-setting sabotage against government installations, as well as its selective terrorism against the Armed Forces and the Political Forces.

It will attempt to infiltrate the institutions of the Armed Forces and the Political Forces. It will carry out harassment and reconnaissance with respect to military installations in order to obtain information.

It will increase the work of winning over and recruiting the population, especially among students (high school and university), workers and the unemployed.

It will maintain its intimidation campaign against political and neighborhood authorities and intensify the campaign to reduce the prestige of the Government and the Armed Forces, using front organizations in the exterior that present the Shining Path as the defender of the cause of the just social change.

For its part, the MRTA will seek to build its organization by recruiting political members coming from the rest of the left, with the goal of pursuing the struggle within its strategic conception of "winning over the masses," increasing its presence in the rest of the country.

It will seek cooperation with the Shining Path in the armed struggle and will call upon the Marxist-Leninist groups to form the Popular Revolutionary Movement (MPR) with the goal of carrying out the "Popular Democratic Revolution."

It will favor the creation of the National Popular Assembly so as to take advantage of the mobilization of leaders that have influence over sectors of the population.

On the international level, it will continue with the contacts and coordination with subversive groups throughout the continent and with its sources of external financing.

n. URUGUAY

After a period of prohibited existence and an almost total lack of organization (1976/1980), leftist organizations began a slow but permanent process of attempting to reconquer lost ground, reunify, keep alive the idea of revolution and transform themselves politically in a possibility as a "government with real power" in 1989.

In order for this to be possible, they had to confront a number of intervening obstacles to achieve their first great tactical objective, what subversion calls "fall of the dictatorship," an indispensable condition for the development of its subsequent trajectory.

The organizations which in the past have carried out armed struggle and those which comprised its political front, once recovering their legality, put new strategies into practice which came out of a deep self-criticism around the revolutionary process carried out in URUGUAY in the '60s and '70s.

The principal points of self-criticism have to do with the excessive growth of the military wing while neglecting the mass fronts, which caused the organizations to lack the necessary popular support and, upon suffering military defeats, to end up totally isolated.

Therefore, the current strategy contemplates taking advantage of the "spring-like democracy" which the country is living in order to carry out essential mass work that will permit them to gain support in the population through direct action or through the Popular Movement and the trade union, social and neighborhood organizations that constitute it.

These plans are followed by all organizations, but in particular the Uruguayan Communist Party (PCU), the National Liberation Movement-Tupamaros (MLN-T), the 26th of March Movement (M-26 March) and the Party for the People's Victory (PVP), which are the principal revolutionary groups.

The PCU has worked intensively in the last two years under the slogan "Advance in Democracy," succeeding, in the first place, in rebuilding its mass of affiliates, adjusting its financing and developing a financial organization as well as an organization of self-defense or security. It should be pointed out that the growth in the number of members during this time is significant.

On the international level, the PCU considers it an opportune moment to encourage propaganda with respect to the "peace offensive" of the USSR, and secondly, to back the democratic upsurge at the continental level.

The MLN-T, since the freeing of their principal leaders, is involved in creating a new image, particularly among the youth, to which end it carries out a profound work among the masses.

o. VENEZUELA

The activity of the Marxist-Leninist groups is currently directed toward carrying out mass work and not military operations.

The subversive groups that in this moment are most active are the Red Flag (BR) and VENCEREMOS (V) (We Will Win) which began an offensive in March 1987 which continues to the present.

Currently, VENEZUELA is experiencing the resurgence of subversion due to the opportune political moment offered it by the delicate social and political situation of the country.

In this area, both the BR and the V are dedicated to bringing together the other leftist and ultra-leftist political parties in order to carry out acts of violence.

The BR and V strategy is directed toward inciting the people to rebel against the government and the system, and they have been developing broad mass and proselytizing work, using legal front organizations which take care of political and propaganda, as well as organizational work.

The mass work is directed at the student population, both high school and university, the workers and the poorer masses, which generally come together in neighborhood organizations.

Subversive work is observed in protests, marches, strikes, symbolic and propagandistic land seizures and speeches full of slogans which discredit the government.

These activities begin in a peaceful form and end up as violence. This forces the government to take security measures to maintain order in the country.

The Third National Convention of the MLN-T held in December, 1986 established some outlines which are still in effect. Among others, armed struggle was ratified as the most probable road to the taking of power. It was also decided that members would be trained in violent measures. The concept of "continentality," launched in a timely manner (1967) by the Conference of the Organization of Latin American States, was maintained.

Strategically, the final objective of "national liberation" was reaffirmed as the first phase of the Socialist revolution. In the area of politics, the creation of a "large front" that can widen alliances, with the idea of isolating the government, is sought. With respect to methods, the Movement decided that it will be flexible in the tactical and firm in the strategic.

The work of the MLN-T with respect to the Armed Forces has a double objective:

1) To work toward lowering its prestige with the population through a campaign of denunciations;

2) To create a fracture within the Armed Forces through agitation and confrontations between civilian and official personnel.

The M-26 is a fraction which broke away from the MLN-T, ideologically controlled by the PCU. It has an enormous quantity of money and infrastructure (businesses, supermarkets, drug stores, printing houses, etc.). It maintains a very radicalized stance. It is very well organized and its activity is permanent.

It has created front organizations with the aim of influencing youth, children, women, and in general in the cultural area.

The great sum of money that it possesses has its origins in careful financial and commercial investment carried out in the exterior (SWEDEN) during the years it was a clandestine organization.

Also notable is the coordination among all the leftist and ultra-leftist sectors to carry out activities established by the "National Work Plan for the Masses" which is being carrying out exactly as it was foreseen by the DTBs. The purpose is to combine and coordinate actions, and seek a leader for the entire left which can represent it in the next electoral process.

4. Conclusions

a. The World Situation

1) The USSR still maintains the initiative through the strategy of Revolutionary War.

2) Subversion continues to promote terrorist actions with the aim of achieving its objectives, with a resurgence of extremist activity in the principal security areas of the West.

3) On the other hand, subversion, using its mobility, political appearance and mimicry of legal organizations, seeks to complement armed struggle through participation and political infiltration.

4) The "political means" used by Marxism constitute an adaptation to new forms of struggle.

5) The USSR has demonstrated, as has been evidenced, a political-terrorist subversive capability in its plans developed in EUROPE.

6) The subversive-terrorist war of attrition on the European continent, a vital area for the world and Western security, has been directed toward achieving the participation of the USSR in Western interests and creativity.

7) The Marxist-Leninist strategy of "political means" becomes relevant in the penetration and/or participation in the traditional European political institutions, by means of Eurocommunism and the circumstantial support of terrorism.

8) The neo-communists (European, American, African) create new forms of spreading communism that are more "trustworthy" methods for the West, at the same time that international terrorism has been structured on

the basis of an interconnected network of national and international movements.

9) The worldwide DTBs do not act in isolation. On the contrary, they are led and supported logistically by the USSR and its allies, forming a real "terror international."

10) This "international" unfolds with unusual dynamism and with resources which are more and more sophisticated, contrasting with the disparity in criteria used in the Western world for limiting or impeding the advance of Marxist-Leninist terrorist subversion in all its forms and expressions.

11) On its part, international Marxism takes advantage of the vulnerabilities of the West, as well as the indecision of the hegemonic powers in consolidating a common interaction as a response to communist expansion.

12) Marxism-Leninism currently is engaged in a penetration campaign primarily in the South Pacific (PHILIPPINES), the MIDDLE EAST, AFRICA and LATIN AMERICA.

13) A greater prominence of the Soviet State can be imagined as a result of the campaign of MIKHAIL GORBACHOV's campaign to demonstrate an opening and transparency, tending to neutralize the United States and reach a position that would be more acceptable for the West.

14) This "new policy" of the Soviet leader can be translated, at the same time, into a hardening of the action of local communist parties to gain positions of power, and not limit themselves to mere electoral participation.

15) The "opening" does not include the elimination of the doctrine of Soviet social-imperialism.

GORBACHOV's new political, social and economic positions tend to solve communism's serious economic problems in accord with the world's challenges, and modernizing the methods of world conquest and/or participation in international control.

b. The Continental Situation

1) Soviet-Cuban penetration is a reality that is reflected in the strengthening of Sandinismo, which constitutes a serious danger for the security of communication lanes: the CARIBBEAN and the PACIFIC OCEAN.

2) The NICARAGUAN situation involves the other Central American and Caribbean nations, opens up the threat of the consolidation of a center of international communism which is complemented by CUBA in order to achieve the triangulation of the CARIBBEAN.

3) The Communist-Castroist strategy is projected with bellicose violence toward EL SALVADOR, GUATEMALA and HONDURAS, destabilizing the area in an attempt to close the ANTILLEAN ARC.

4) North America (because of its geostrategic position) and the countries of the SOUTHERN CONE (for their economic potential), constitute the principal political-economic objectives of interest to the USSR, without abandoning direct or indirect action through the Continent's Solidarity Organizations, generating tensions in the area.

5) The political and social imbalances that the South American nations face are many; but, to a greater or lessor degree, they suffer communist action in its political or armed form, or a combination of the two, which surreptitiously establishes the infrastructure for future ideological conquest under the theme of "national liberation."

6) Eurocommunism on the continental level, in the form of American communism, can be seen in the leftist penetration and Gramscian position adapted in a national and popular way.

7) To the degree that the extremist organizations suspect the impossibility of achieving power by armed struggle, they choose to create legal or pseudo-legal mechanisms to penetrate political-cultural institutions and/or peace agreements framed within the strategy of "war of pacification."

c. The Particular Situation in Each Country

1) ARGENTINA

The complete subversive political spectrum is heading toward the adoption of the Sandinista revolutionary model.

The makeup of this front is indispensable to a strategy that contemplates action through a political front and another, interdependent military one, where the entire left is brought together.

In general, nevertheless, in the subversive political spectrum shows a marked tendency toward armed struggle, evidenced by the DTBs and in the Marxist Political Organizations, taking advantage of the economic and psychosocial situation.

2) BOLIVIA

The International Communist Movement considers this country to be the heart of South America for spreading communism to the United States.

For the moment, subversion has chosen indirect action, political and social agitation, and infiltration and control of the left in view of the political weakening experienced by the right-wing parties.

While no solutions to the socio-economic problems are given, social agitation will be the banner for the Anarcho-Sindicalist political line.

3) BRAZIL

The left continues to infiltrate the Federal, State, and Municipal Administrations and political parties, aided by the progressive church.

At the same time, a radicalized opposition to the constitutional government is developing, which tends toward its destabilization.

On the other hand, subversion continues to prepare its members to carry out armed struggle.

The government and the Armed Forces are in agreement in a direct action against everything which threatens to violate national security.

4) COLOMBIA

To the degree that subversion develops by applying the process of "prolonged popular war" the country will continue to experience difficult times.

Despite the governmental program of reconciliation, it is unlikely that the armed groups will cease their objective of achieving power by means of armed struggle.

5) CHILE

Marxism-Leninism insists on using insurrectional means and its activities are directed toward provoking a political crisis in 1989, using the excuse of the illegality of the plebescite.

The specific area of subversion and terrorism is that of the political and basically subversive level, since, with the promulgation of the new Constitution of 1980, the Communist Party, declared illegal, could do nothing more than support the insurrectional road.

6) ECUADOR

Subversion is developing and carries out political and armed propaganda, with limited direct or indirect support of the leftist political parties, union, teacher and student sectors and the "progressive clergy."

Subversive activity takes advantage of the legal circumstances in that the Ecuadoran legislation lacks an anti-terrorist law.

7) EL SALVADOR

Subversion has decided that the process of revolutionary struggle consists of the establishment of the mass political army of the revolution through the National Union of Salvadoran Workers, inscribed within the political line of the FMLN.

The Marxist-Leninist leaders have constructed a struggle based on prolonged popular war and the intensive development of class struggle.

8) UNITED STATES

With respect to direct subversion against the United States, the intelligence directed toward weakening the highest levels of North American security is the most relevant.

This threat is made concretized in the psychological actions, espionage, disinformation and manipulation of the media, which the USSR carries out covertly or through third countries.

9) GUATEMALA

The combined action of subversive groups relies on violence to achieve the isolation of, and the confrontation between, the government and the army.

They persist in ideologically destroying the image of the army and infiltrating the private and church sectors, State Organizations, pressure groups and the media.

At the same time, the Subversive Terrorist Organizations continue clandetine organizing of urban and rural political-military cells in order to reincorporate them into the armed struggle.

10) HONDURAS

While it is true that the Terrorist Organizations were, in large part practically annihilated, it must be noted that the radicalized sectors of the country could attempt to reinitiate armed activity.

They could take advantage of opportune moments, such as the indecision around the Sandinista problem, and the ideological-political controversies with neighboring countries.

11) PANAMA

Subversive activity, launched by the Communist Party is confined by the attitude of the Defense Forces, and by the traditional anti-communism of the religious people, who reject communist doctrine as a system of life.

12) PARAGUAY

The subversive spectrum in the country is in a preparatory phase for armed struggle, with scant possibilities for achieving power.

Faced with internal limitations, the possibility that subversion is seeking out external support cannot be ruled out.

Currently, subversion operates on the political level, using infiltration and/or participation; no armed subversive organization has been detected.

13) PERU

Subversion developed by the PCP-SL organizations and the MRTA are directed primarily toward achieving greater political presence, in order to influence national and international public opinion.

The subversive tendency of the leaders is to maintain the initiative by neutralizing or surpassing the successes of the counter-subversive strategy of the government.

This objective contemplates a greater geographic sphere of control, greater political activity, propaganda and terrorism in remote Andean communities.

This strategy does not mean that both organizations have abandoned the methods or forms of armed struggle, but that they seek opportune moments to re-initiate their activities according to preconceived plans.

They are currently continuing with the preparation and training of their members and enlarging the "Popular Guerrilla Army."

14) URUGUAY

In accordance with the new strategies adopted by the subversive organizations after their legalization in March of 1985, their political proposals are directed toward:

a) Recovering political ground among the population by means of profound mass political work, tending toward achieving the control over civilian society.

b) Taking advantage of the legal and political framework currently in effect to develop mass work and create alliances with non-Marxist sectors to broaden political spaces and ability to maneuver.

In synthesis, the subversive slogan is "advance in democracy, organize and educate," without discarding the opportunity to take up armed struggle.

15) VENEZUELA

An increase in urban subversion has been noted.

The leftist and ultra-leftist sectors are trying to unite forces against the government and the democratic system.

The strategy of the Terrorist Organizations is to develop mass work among students and workers, using the government's economic and political measures as a base and countering with cultural-propagandistic activity.

The leftist sectors direct and lead peaceful protests.

There is a real combination of political subversion with preparation for armed struggle.

Probable Trajectory

a. In General

1) International communism will continue to promote subversive movements and their offensive methods utilizing especially the tactic of "peaceful coexistence," stressing winning over the masses, exploiting social and economic conditions.

2) "Armed action" will not be discarded, but the places where it will be applied, and its limits, will depend directly on the ability of the Armed Forces of each country to react and neutralize it.

3) Communism will attempt to disrupt the economy of the Western countries and impede their economic integration at the continental or regional level, with the goal of hindering their even-handed and harmonioas development.

4) Subversion will attempt by all means to seek unity among the various groups which, led by distinct tendencies, operate independently.

5) An indirect maneuver over WESTERN EUROPE will be evident. Two-thirds of the energy resources that industry needs comes from the NEAR and MIDDLE EAST and the raw materials particularly from AFRICA.

6) It is estimated that communism could come to destabilize governments which are of interest to the USSR, applying a dual policy: promoting its ideology on the one hand, and, on the other, creating or improving diplomatic and/or commercial relations, with the goal of guaranteeing a consciousness disposed to infiltration.

7) Marxism-Leninism will continue to penetrate Western public opinion through disinformation:

a) Driving forward the theme of pacification in the context of peaceful coexistence, and accusing detractors of being enemies of peace.

b) Insulting the capitalist countries for their world economic backwardness and for the social imbalance generated by poverty.

c) Associating the concept of the human liberation with that of the Theology of Liberation, which has gained followers in the last decade.

8) The USSR's global strategy will continue with its practice of Western penetration, espionage, counter-intelligence, technology transfer, tending to reduce United States influence and inhibiting military actions to contain international communism.

9) The USSR, at the same time, will promote and intensify the strategy of tension in conflictive areas in relation to the strategic interests of the leading Western countries, the United States, Europe and Japan.

b. In Relation to America

1) Subversion, with international support, will continue to act all over the continent, placing emphasis on supporting disorganized movements with the aim of once again giving them a capacity for struggle.

2) Marxism will exploit to its advantage all reasons for agitation which are a result of existing imbalances, and will do so through the use of trained agitators.

3) Subversive threats with respect to AMERICA could develop in the following way:

a) In the Political Sphere

(1)   International communism will continue its support with the aim of increasing its prestige on the continent, looking to extend its influence.

(2)   It will continue the permanent activity of communist parties in support of terrorism and political subversion.

(3)   Subversion will try, by means of political activities, to interfere in the internal affairs of the countries of the continent.

(4)   It will continue with its campaign to lower the prestige of the governments that are most decisive in combatting subversion, and the prestige of United States foreign policy toward the rest of the continent.

(5)   It will try to form and strengthen political fronts with different parties with Marxist ideologies and/or infiltrated by international communism.

(6)   It will create favorable conditions for producing friction and distancing between governments and their people, by means of exploiting the theme of human rights.

(7)   The activities of political-terrorist subversion will continue to be a threat for the nascent democracies of the continent.

(8)   Narco-terrorism will continue to constitute a method of subversion for political corruption.

b) In the Social Sphere

(1)   Exploiting the existing conditions in the countries that have not reached development, in order to capitalize on the economic and cultural diffe-

rences of the various social groups with the aim of obstructing the actions of governments and facilitating ideological penetration.

(2) Encouraging the growth of "progressive groups" in the church, with the aim of reaching the masses by using issues of social satisfaction and class struggle.

(3) The infiltration and control of student and worker's organizations will continue to be a priority objective.

(4) Subversion will try to continue influencing educational systems, to continue indoctrination of youth from the first years of school.

c) In the Economic Sphere

(1) The possibility and necessity of widening markets and credits with the communist countries will facilitate ideological penetration.

(2) Subversion will launch an open or disguised economic war with the aim of bringing development plans to a halt, looking to widen the gaps that exist between the different social classes and to increase agitation.

(3) It will try to impede the implementation of international economic agreements that tend to improve the standard of living of the inhabitants of the continent, using the tactic of encouraging economic nationalism.

(4) The International Communist Movement will try to take the greatest possible advantage of the poor economic situation of the majority of the Latin American countries and their marginilaized masses, disposing them to insurrection as a consequence of a

national and international policy fraught with
uncertainty.

d) In the Military Sphere

(1)   The various guerrilla and terrorist movements will continue to receive the support and leadership of international subversive organizations.

(2)   The degree of dependence of some countries on
communist bloc nations will increase, through
technical advice and arms sales.

(3)   The infiltration and ideological indoctrination campaign in the Armed Forces will continue.

(4)   Military alliances among the countries of
the continent will be obstructed, placing emphasis on
anti-subversive agreements.

(5)   The strategic plan that motivates the
greatest coordination and unity of military action by
Terrorist Organizations, led by the USSR and supported by CUBA, NICARAGUA and LIBYA, will advance.

DOCUMENT III:
STRATEGY
OF THE
INTERNATIONAL COMMUNIST
MOVEMENT (ICM)
IN LATIN AMERICA
THROUGH VARIOUS MODES
OF ACTION

Document III: Strategy of the International Communist Movement (ICM) in Latin America, Through Various Modes Action

I. Introduction

Presently, the nature and mode of operation of the Soviet project is seen in the most diverse areas of politics, law and culture. Through intelligence efforts aimed at understanding ICM actions and objectives, the importance of its great indirect strategic maneuver and its permanent revision of methodology to take advantage of and use different forms of penetration, infiltration and domination is no longer hidden.

Certainly at no level of the political, business, trade union, cultural and, obviously military managemnet can we plead ignorance regarding the fundamental lines of the expansionist Communist project, that the USSR orients and finances in a perticularly hegemonic way. This knowledge, open or not, is part of international reality and of own vicissitudes of all western governments. They must operate with this knowlege in order to consolidate or conserve a type of life based on liberty.

In consequence, we do not here reiterate already familiar concepts. Instead, we allow ourselves, in this XVII Conference, to reflect upon some ICM courses of action that seem to us decisive, because they get to the bottom of its capacit to harm those very principles that give life to our concept of the world. They redefine these values for their own ends; and, in short, relativize and empty them of all community and personal meaning.

In this context, our thoughts are centered especially on some of the sectoral stategies of this long standing operative modality of the USSR, also seen in the area of international relations as a concurrent aspect of its so called " Double-Keyboard Policy". On the one hand they sign peace treaties or take part in negotiations conforming to International Law, while on the other they employ subversive action and terrorism in all areas to achieve their objectives.

It is fitting to note at this point that the present GLASNOST (politicy of openness and transparency) of GORBACHOV, according to our preliminary interpretation, is one more modality of this general strategy, although of an important political subtlety. This is due, among other things, to the prospective necessities of internal fortification and the accommidation of new technological challenges.

In accordance with this, we will determine some conspicuous moments in the type and incidence of this mode of operation; at first, in the framework of the continent's religious experience, and in the doctrinal development of Liberation Theology (LT). This, we feel, is a relevant social reality of our countries that we cannot avoid considering in order to clearly appreciate the reality in which we are living. Then we will note some of the coordinated actions of the Marxist Revolutionary Organizations in realtion to the different solidaritiy entities that have penetrated into the midst of civil society.

II. Observations About Sectorial Strategy in Latin America

a. The Marxist Variants in Liberation Theology

POPE JOHN PAUL II opportunely expressed (Dec. 21, 1984) before the Cardinals and Prelates of the Roman Curia, that Liberation Theology uses the suffering of the poor as a pretext for a new type of "oppression, sometimes more serious." The fact that the dominant motivation for the Catholic Church's pastoral action is the "preferential option for the poor" does not mean it must "confuse itself with a reduction of the poor to abstract social-political or economic categories."

For us, these Pontifical affirmations clearly summarize the pastoral style of the church's actions in LATIN AMERICA, and the doctrinal problem produced by deviating from the meaning that sustains the committed purpose of this action. Or exposition tries to increase understanding of this phenomenon and, at the same time, rescue the uncompromising line in a more subtle and substantive way, from ICM penetration.

1) General Characterization

a) Review of historical aspects

The theological movement we know as LT brings together interests, objectives and activities of a vast sector of the Catholic Church, and a good part of important Protestant nuclei. This movement was born towards the end of the 1960's in response to the uneasiness generated by the second Vatican (Vatican II) Council, especially in pastoral and social areas. Vatican II's recommendations were adapted and applied to the realities and necessities of LATIN AMERICA by the Latin American bishops, in the pastoral work of the Assembly of MEDELLIN (CELAM, COLUMBIA, 1968) and in successive meetings.

This current extended itself in other third world countries in response to similar changes. This does not mean that the categories or modalities of thought that served as the basis of development for this position arose from reality; rather, from the use (usually out of context) of European categories of thought, as will be seen later.

The first conspicuous, systematic attempt to conceptually organize the new theological reflections – in terms later questioned by the Congregation for the Doctrine of the Faith – was the July 1968 conference held by the National Meeting of the Clerical Movement (National Independent Organization of Priests), held in CHIMBOTE (PERU), by the priest and theologian GUSTAVO GUTIERREZ on the theme: "Toward a Theology of Liberation." In 1971, this same priest published a book entitled "Theology of Liberation," which served as the basis for new doctrinal developments of the question. GUTIERREZ's book has been published in 10 Spanish editions and has been translated into nine languages, generating a movement around this subject that had repercussions in almost all Third World countries with Catholic or Christian populations, and in some important theological and political circles in EUROPE, including the VATICAN.

The Third General Latin American Bishops' Conference CELAM-III, 1979) warned that "theological reflection is exposed to the risk of ideologization, when it starts from the practice of Marxist analysis" and concluded that "the consequences are the total politicization of Christian existence, the dissolution of the language of faith into that of social sciences, and an emptying of the transcendental dimension of Christian salvation" (DOCUMENT OF PUEBLA, 545).

By then, many of the new theological developments had given way to doctrinal confusion, to explicit support of violent methods for changing serious structural socio-economic problems, and to the creation, in the Christian environment, of the necessity of generating changes through instruments used by Marxist subversion to realize their objectives.

The crystallizations of the political-ideological deviations, presupposed in the development of these radicalized foci of LT, was quickly seen in the manipulations of the Nicaraguan regime. This distortion, that also promotes the installation of parallel teachings and breaks the doctrinal and institutional unity of church, was repeatedly condemned by different organs and ecclesiastic documents in the country and throughout the continent and by the POPE himself on various occasions. (See, among others, the conclusions of the Theology Meeting of Managua, 8/16. Sept. 80).

b) Clarification of some conceptual aspects

The expression Liberation Theology does not, in itself, constitute a motive for dispute. Certainly, the theme of liberation and the theological reflection found in LT has a Biblical base and fits perfectly within the most genuine apostolic tradition and teachings of the church.

What is interesting in this discussion is the conceptual systemization that intentionally distorts the orientation of these teachings, supported in the "preferential option for the poor"; examining the biblical theme of liberation, its urgency, and the necessity of its practical realization using non-Christian structures of thought or analytical categories, including, in some cases, definitely anti-Christian ones. In this sense, some lines of reflection of LT directly identify the Christian message with the Marxist project of liberation; they uncritically assume the analytical variables of that ideology as "scientific methodology" and upon these foundations develop new theological readings. It is doctrinally valid to read politics from the perspective of the Gospel, that is, of faith itself, but not the other way around.

The document of PUEBLA (#559) confirms our assertion and adds, referring to these groups, that "the temptation is to identify the Christian message with an ideology and submit it to the latter, inviting a rereading of the Gospel beginning with a political option" (also see 561 and 543/546 and JOHN PAUL II, in his Inaugural Speech)

The interpretation of this type of LT transformed the "preferential option for the poor" into a concept far from the meaning of the faith, in agreement with the Marxist idea of "class struggle as the path toward a society without classes," emptying it of its fundamental Christian, ecclesiastical, and pastoral content. In this way, this modality of theological reflection reduces, among other aspects, the figure of JESUS to that of a political and social leader and establishes, in the womb of the church, the dialectic contradiction of Marxism itself with the choice between the popular and the hierarchical church, as a representation of the struggle between oppressed and oppressors. In this focus the sense of being Christian is homologous with a determined party militancy and the effective participation in the struggle to impose a new social order promoted by Marxist socialism.

2) Scheme of the Different Currents of Liberation Theology

Different classifications of LT exist. They all attempt to distinguish and rescue the substantive elements that enliven a genuine, necessary theological reflection that can serve as the design for and

help create a ministry able to meet current social
and political challenges.

Another common element of these classifications is
that, in general, their authors respond to a vocation
inspired in the unity of the church and its
teachings. It can be said that they are attempts to
overcome the doctrinal deviations produced in the
first developments.

The classifying criteria they promote is the basic
distinction between the variations of Liberation
Theology whose starting point is "religious" or the
"experience of the sacred" and those that put
emphasis and initial motivation on the "political-
social" or in " determinations of the profane" and
that, therefore, have become effective channels of
Marxist diffusion and indoctrination. The latter
were condemned on repeated occasions by diverse organisms and ecclesiastical sectors. They constitute,
in the context of this exposition, what we call
"Marxist variants of LT" (See, among others documents, that produced by the Team of Pastoral Theological Reflection CELAM, BOGOTA, Nov. 73).

With the intent of systemizing and briefly charac-
terizing these currents we will point out, in the
first place, the reflection efforts founded on a
religious basis, which we will call "bishops'
pastoral" proposed by Cardinal LOPEZ TRUJILLO
(Colombian, former secretary general of CELAM).
Then, we will summarize the more radical positions
that correspond to a process of manipulation of the
faith or which facilitate the elimination of its
essential content. Among these, we will identify a
more moderate tendency that, in its attempts to
articulate the facts of religious experience, continues to hierarchize the socio-political factors and
the supposedly "scientific" and aseptic contribution
of Marxism.

a) Bishops' Pastoral Current

This line of reflection finds a source of orientation in MEDELLIN (1986). Some of its leading representatives are the aforementioned Cardinal EDUARDO PIRONIO. In trying to differentiate itself from the general denomination, some expositors have employed terms such as "theology from the pastoral practice of the church" or "theology of the liberation of culture." These different attempts are made within the framework of the orientation of the Magisterium and in conformity with the principle of basing all reflection on the religious experience of the people; in other words, in the theological practice of this Magisterium that allows for a deepened sense of the evangelistic mission to meet new demands, without losing sight of the history and culture of the people of the continent. (See JOHN PAUL II, Inaugural Speech of Puebla, 1979, and other episcopal documents). The following words of Cardinal LOPEZ TRUJILLO himself eloquently synthesize the essential inspiration of this current: "The accent is deliberately placed on the religious, without forgetting the political dimension, but without giving it such a privileged position that it appears as the fundamental concern. This current has numerous expressions in pastoral meeting, articles, episcopal documents, pastoral letters, etc. I has served"--he concludes--"to encourage a new and positive pastoral presence."

b) Moderate Marxist Current.

Even though this current does not formally deny the common religious bases, the determining character of the Marxist instruments of analysis it uses and the priority consequently given to socio-political aspects as the basis of that ideological formulation, have placed the role of faith in a secondary position.

The religious aspect, while not being entirely excluded, is at least inevitably absorbed or distorted by anti-Christian presuppositions, despite that fact that this current's followers try to separate that which they consider the "scientific" support of Marxism used for the working out of pastoral theology and reject the explicit atheism and dogmatic materialism of their ideas about man and history.

Without a doubt, this dangerous ambiguity of doctrinal procedure and treatment makes them fall into the fallacy of trying, on one side, to back off from the imperatives of Marxist action—and at the same time to emphasize the all but uncritical use of the categories of Marxist analysis.

In this position are, for example, GUSTAVO GUTIERREZ and ENRIQUE DUSSEL, with differences of tone, and those who, like them, search for a "combination" with Marxism, in the illusory, restricted sense mentioned before. Other important theologians, like the Argentinean LUCIO GERA, have warned that this "combination" is neither possible nor congruent without affecting the essence of theological reflection.

Despite these internal contradictions, the concrete application of those postulates gave rise to the formation of different movements, made up of priests, religious and lay persons, such as: "Priest for LATIN AMERICA," in COLOMBIA; "Movement of Priests for the Third World," in ARGENTINA; "Christians for Socialism," in CHILE; "National Independent Organization of Priests," in PERU; "Movement of Priestly Reflection," in ECUADOR, "Priests for the People," in MEXICO.

Many of the participants succumbed, consciously or not, to the obvious conditioning imposed by choosing the conceptual instrument of Marxism; therefore, their initial positions as reflected in pastoral expressions (sermons, works, writings) were radicalized to the detriment of the truths of the faith and ecclesiastical meaning.

The most moderate version's arguments and attitudes involving sociopolitical data were derived from the idea that it is necessary to redeem social demands in the Latin American framework through an appeal to the "Dependence Theory." Ecclesiastical structures were denied, since they were identified, along with dominant structures, economic dependence and capital, as the cause of the oppression of the poor. Starting from these ideas, the most radical positions justify the class struggle. For them, no truth exists without revolutionary combat to destroy the dominant classes: the violence of the rich must be met by the revolutionary counter-violence of the poor.

One eloquent example that allows us to observe this progressive adherence to the ICM project and its modes of operation is the following quote from the conclusions of the Meeting of 1975, in ECUADOR, attended by several bishops, including Monseigneur MENDEZ ARCEO, bishop of CUERNAVACA (MEXICO): "It is necessary to adopt the instrument of Marxist analysis and promote the taking of political power by the proletariat...maintain the ideological struggle with the hierarchy, reject the anti-Marxist, anti-Communist and anti-revolutionary position; it is necessary to go deeper into liberation theology (obviously in those terms); propitiate the emergence of the popular church and be in solidarity with the bishops who support it. ..."

c) Marxist current

The deliberate use of Marxist method and philosophy (which are inseparable) along with a subversive practice in the bosom of the ecclesiastical community itself, as well as that of society, has ended up placing some liberation theologians visibly outside the Catholic Church.

One significant representative of this position is HUGO ASSMAN, Brazilian, doctor of theology and with a Master's degree in sociology, who opportunely has worked as the secretary of the Institute of Church and Society in LATIN AMERICA (ISAL). This representative, author of "Theology from the Practice of Liberation," has publicly expressed his Marxist ideological affiliation. Also aligned with this current are some who have, by their attitudes and modes of operation, marginalized themselves from serious theological discussion; among them are RUBEM ALVES, Brazilian Protestant intellectual who abandoned the Presbyterian faith; Chilean priest reduced to a lay status PABLO RICHARD; Chilean priests ROLANDO MUNOZ, SEGUNDO GALILEA, and SERGIO TORRES; Panamanian IGNACIO ELLACURIA; Guatemalan JOSE HERNANDEZ PICO; theologian J. COMBLIN, known by his book "Theology of Revolution," among others.

Certainly, these positions no longer respond to the original spirit of renovation and pastoral adaptation of MEDELLIN or PUEBLA; one cannot even say they constitute doctrinal errors. Rather they are a conscious assumption and manipulation of the truly liberating Christian message of salvation to further the objectives of the Communist revolution.

For this reason, the timely reaction of the Sacred Congregation of the Faith, with its two Instructions that we will analyze later, and the dispute sustained in the ecclesiastical environment tend to underline the incongruity of this combination of Marxist "science" and theology.

In this respect it is interesting to mention the reflection of another well-known theologian, P. ALBERTO METHOL FERRE, Uruguayan. This "combination," he says,"is something that deviates from the roots of

MARX, ENGELS, LENIN, GRAMSCI, etc. Marx, Engels,
etc. don't even imagine this combination could be
possible. It is understood, with coherence, because
the incoherent is always possible. In the MARX and
LENIN would share the opinion of the Magisterium: it
is not possible to divide Marxist philosophy from its
science, the method from the content. ...Marxists
consider the "combination" of theology and "Marxist
method unfeasible. Nevertheless" he adds, "they
applaud those who make or proclaim the feasibility of
this 'combination.' Why this apparent incongruency
of the Marxists?"--he asks himself--"Very simple.
For them the 'combination ' is indicative of the
penetration Marxism in the church. It is indicative
that they believe that in this 'combination' the
hegemonic element is 'Marxist science' and not theology," which is actually what happened in the two
currents we are analyzing. "In this way," he continues, "the Marxists call any criticism of this
'combination,' 'reactionary' from 'progressive,' they
are evidently congruent in eulogizing the incongruent
'combination' of some theologians. The Soviet press
openly speaks of this theology of liberation that
combines with Marxism. And from there comes the
worldwide campaign against Ratzinger." He refers to
Cardinal JOSEPH RATZINGER, eminent theologian,
Prefect of the Congregation for the Doctrine of the
Faith, who edited the Instructions of the VATICAN
about this subject. (See the Magazine NEXO, 2nd
trimester, 1986, No. 8, p. 5).

3) The Church's Response

The Church clarified the terms of the dispute pro-
voked in its midst and reoriented theological
reflection and pastoral action, fundamentally in two
instructions that, as we have said, were edited by
Cardinal J. RATZINGER and backed by Pope JOHN PAUL
II.

a) First Instruction

The First Instruction of the Congregation for the Doctrine of the Faith of September, 1984 was "Concerning Some Aspects of Liberation Theology." As P. METHOL FERRE expresses (see cited article); "its essential problem was whether the aforementioned 'composition' with Marxism was coherent with the Catholic faith." He considered "some aspects" of "some currents" without mentioning any names.

The document continued the orientation of the Encyclical Letter "OCTOGESIMA ADVENIENS" (1970) in which PAUL VI referred to the relation between Marxism and Catholic Christianity.

Its main goal was to warn the faithful about doctrinal deviations originating in scientifically based interpretations of the realities of faith and demands of a predetermined social and political practice, that leads to neglect of the specific mission of the Church's pastors. In summary, it was essentially critical and responded negatively to the uncritical attempts of a combination with Marxism.

The abbreviated version of the VATICAN document is divided into six articles, the content of which we summarize:

1) It defines the term "Liberation Theology" as a theological and pastoral movement. It realizes that the great number of religious and laypersons inspired by or par ticipating in it are "not always capable of adequately stating its content." It affirms, in con tinuation, that some theologians of "LT" have put "in circulation a series of ideas ruinous for the faith." This situation has brought about the need for cla rification by the Magisterium.

2) The document distinguishes between the legitimate and necessary aspirations of the poor to achieve dignified lives, in conformity with the Christian sense of human, and the theological expressions that give rise to this aspiration. Of the latter, "some are authentic, others ambiguous and others. . .represent a serious danger to the faith and to the theological and moral life of Christians."

3) The ecclesiastical document wants to address the problem in a positive way, since "Liberation is a Christian theme based on Biblical foundations, in both the Old and New Testaments. There is a specific liberty of Christianity. CHRIST is our liberator." From this perspective "Liberation Theology" can be understood "in a completely positive way, if accent is put on certain aspects of the Mystery and on pastoral consequences, and not substituted for the theology of the Mystery."

In this regard it mentions reiterated pronouncements of the Magisterium. Among these the message of the Pope in PUEBLA stands out, which "outlined the coordinates of all authentic Liberation Theology: truth about the Church, truth about man." Here the preferential option for the poor finds its profound and legitimate meaning.

4) "Precisely"--he says in his fourth article--"in the name of this option, interpreted in a seriously deviate way, certain theologians have spread mistakes, ruinous for the faith, about which the document proposes to call the attention of pastors and the faithful."

Nevertheless, it is recognized that behind these errors is "the will to fight against the misery of the people," and the idea of appealing to scientific diagnosis as a fundamental condition for effectiveness. Both intentions are just in themselves, although errors appear "when, without critical examination, this analysis is identified with Marxism. It is not realized that this depends ideological premises intrinsically incompatible with the Christian faith." This, without a doubt, leads to the perversion of Christianity.

Thus, for example, the document underlines a certain number of supposition;

a) the concept of truth that dominates all theological inspiration, taken from Marxism, states that true consciousness is a partisan consciousness., "There is only truth in, by and for revolutionary practice. Through adaptations of language, the radical theologies of liberation adopt a concept similar to the truth, marked by relativism and the primacy of action."

b) The assumption of the "class struggle" category for socio-historical analysis. If one realizes that the concept of history is one of the key concepts of the new liberation theologies, the uncritical use of tis Marxist category drags these theological reflections "toward an immanentism and historicism that affects even the very notion of GOD." It leads to the affirmation that there is only "one history," "rejecting the distinction between the history of salvation and profane history;" history and the "combat that is begun in its name" are made divine.

c) In conditioning theological reflection to political criteria, the only possible analysis is to reduce the meaning of "expressions such as Church of the poor or Church of the people," to "Church of class." With this the unity of the church is denied, "the positions of the hierarchy" are discredited beforehand, and Christians "separated by the class struggle" are even disallowed from "participating in the same eucharistic table."

5) The Marxist influence is also felt in the way theology and its methodology are understood. Thus, "the commitment to struggle for the liberation of the poor, understood in the Marxist sense, becomes the new rule of faith;" the reading of Scripture is "essentially, and often exclusively, a political reading," in which "the radical novelty of the New Testament is cancelled;" the figure of CHRIST is interpreted in a political way, denying his universal redemptive value, and the opposition between the "JESUS of history," and the "JESUS of the faith"; is accepted without criticism; finally, the sacraments become mere symbols of the struggle of the people for liberation.

6) In conclusion, it indicates in what sense one must realize urgent reorientation in the face of a "movement that, although it might intend to serve the poor, cannot fail to lead them to a new misery--the spiritual misery of the loss of faith--and to new slavery."

"The totally politicized conception of Christianity of these theologies leaves the Christian mysteries of the faith and morality without substance."

b) Second Instruction

The "Instruction Concerning Christian Liberty and Liberation" released in April, 1986, completed the Magisterium's task of reorientation on the theme. It constitutes a great synthesis of theology of Catholic history that gathers the essence of Liberation Theology and of the church's teachings and responds to the Pontifical logic of JOHN PAUL II.

The antecedent of this Second Instruction is the Encyclical Letter EVANGELIA NUNTIANDI of PAUL VI, where Evangelism and Liberation are closely united. It is supported, beside, by all the spiritual and intellectual preparation of the entire Church since VATICAN COUNCIL II.

This second document has allowed the possibility for distinct ecclesiastical currents to converge in a general consensus within the bosom of the church. Nevertheless, the worldwide media, in good part controlled directly or indirectly by Marxism, practically silenced the diffusion of this doctrinal synthesis, in contrast to the coverage given the First Instruction, which was aimed at accentuating the differences and the decomposition within the Church.

4) Conclusions about this Modality of Action

As we all know, since MEDELLIN, application of the biblical theme of liberation to social realities of LATIN AMERICA and the THIRD WORLD has had great political resonance due to the role of the church in the region.

Different power groups, and especially Marxism in its multiple varieties, have mobilized to accentuate differences, deepen condemnation and divisions.

From the ecclesiastical point of view, even if this is a temporary, inevitable reality, in the sense that the church is also an institution of the world, it is far from exhausting itself in the relativity of that reality.

In principle, in our opinion, it deals basically with distinguishing the habitual exercise of power of the bishop (who is responsible for the vigilance of the faith, represented at its highest by the POPE), from all ideological maneuvers made by interests both within and outside of the church.

Undoubtedly, the ICM, alerted to the possibility of weakening the power factor and the source of values the church represents, accentuated the contradictions in what it calls "The Religious Front." The disputes generated by the new theological reflection, encouraged intentionally or through neglect by the communication media, constituted an adequate climate for the Marxist penetration of Catholic theology and, in general, Christian practice. The contradictions were accentuated in the strictly doctrinal arena as well as in the permanent promotion of confrontation between the "hierarchy" and "bases." One of the most developed products of this tendency is the so-called "Nicaraguan Theology," the subject of reiterated critical judgements by the General Secretariat of CELAM and of John Paul II.

ROME's strategy to confront this action of Marxist penetration, the emptying of the truths of the faith and the disarticulation of the ecclesiastical structures, was channeled through the firm pastoral action of the POPE himself and of the two instructions of Cardinal J. RATZINGER. The VATICAN'S first maneuver can be considered the dismissal and condemnation of the composition with Marxism, which subtly used the Gramscian modality of formation of a new proletariat consciousness, deepening antagonisms and deviations.

Later, in a second maneuver, he positively affirmed the "nucleus" of Liberation Theology, concerning the basic historical salvation experience of the Universal Church.

In the light of this perfect demarcation between the essential that one must accept, and the Marxist instrumentalization that must be discarded, those who unite the two objectives are self-marginalized.

b. The Coordinated Action
of Revolutionary Marxist Organizations

1) Background

Starting in the 1960's, the ICM developed a specific strategy for Latin America, mounted on the double strategy of subversive action along with an increase of cooperation and technological aid in the area of formal relations. It tried progressively to impose its will on the western world, accentuating regional imbalances. That continental subversive action was centered in CUBA, to which NICARAGUA has been incorporated since the end of the 1970's.

The principal or outstanding characteristic of this mode of operation was violence in its diverse and historic modalities. In the face of the relative failure of this path, the ICM has adjusted its strategy: today it emphasizes cultural action, in conformity with the global lines of thought of ANTONIO GRAMSCI.

a) The Latin American Solidarity Organization (OLAS)

Since the installation of the Communist regime in CUBA, the ICM made numerous attempts to expand the subversive process in Latin America in a coordinated way. One fundamental milestone toward materializing this process was the OLAS, created in HAVANA in 1967.

As we all know, this revolutionary organization was structured on the basis of a multi-national plan, whose final goal was the taking of power through armed struggle throughout our continent.

It is fitting to remember here that 27 "National Committees" participated in the constituting meeting. They advanced "Revolutionary Struggle" as the only way to achieve "liberation." Since then, the CUBAN regime organized diverse multi-national nuclei that gather activists of the extreme left in "Fronts" (cultural, student, trade union, religious, women, etc.), that have contributed to the development of one concurring strategy to political and armed insurrection, through various tactics.

b) Revolutionary Coordinating Junta

Another important moment in the configuration of this strategy was the constitution, in 1973, of the Revolutionary Coordinating Junta (JCR), under the inspiration of the Cuban government.

The Junta was made up of the Revolutionary Army of the People (ERP-Argentina); MLN-Tupamaros (URU-GUAY); Movement of the Revolutionary Left (MIR-CHILE); Movement of the Revolutionary Left (MIR-BOLIVIA); Army of National Liberation (ELN-COLOM-BIA). JCR activities lasted until 1977 without producing the sought-after results. Since then, CUBA has centered its efforts in the destabilization of CENTRAL AMERICA, mainly based on two objective situations: the political juncture of the overthrow of the DTBs of ARGENTINA, CHILE, URUGUAY and BOLIVIA at the hands of the Armed Forces of those countries, and the necessity of quickly creating a Marxist-Leninist base on the American continent itself, which would only be possible within a certain geographical proximity. Consequently, the subversive organizations of NICA-RAGUA, EL SALVADOR and GUATEMALA coordinated their operations. In 1979, the Sandinista Front for National Liberation (FSLN) took power in the first of these countries, from which its activities were projected throughout the whole region.

2) **Conference of Latin American Communist Party**
   General Secretaries

More recently, we have an example of the strategic flexibility of Marxism that explains in good part the "changing objectives," in reality operative adaptation, observed in the framework of the institutional realities of our countries. Thus, on July 1984, the Conference of Latin American Communist Party General Secretaries met in BUENOS AIRES. Delegations from the different CPs throughout the continent participated, along with first-level elements from the USSR, Communist countries of EUROPE, CUBA and NICARAGUA in the role as observers.

During the course of this conference an extensive analysis of Latin American reality was carried out, with the following conclusions;

a) the decade of the '80s marks the beginning of the process of democratization throughout SOUTH AMERICA with the exceptions of CHILE and PARAGUAY.

b) This process was considered positive, based on the possibility that the CP may use this political juncture to grow and insert themselves into society.

Nevertheless, the general situation shows some negative characteristics which the CPs must consider.

1) The democratic governments are in charge of countries whose economies have serious structural distortions.

2) The lowering of international prices on raw materials and the financial burden of the foreign debt sterilized attempts to obtain an adequate level of economic growth and a better distribution of wealth in the different countries.

c) This state of affairs will give way to a new surge of "popular struggles," that will certainly achieve growing levels of organization. Consequently, the CPs conclude that they must put themselves at the forefront of these organizations.

d) Given these premises they consider that the democratic governments will not be able to stop these struggles by increasing the standard of living of the working classes. This will end in situations of repression, and the armed forces will again play an ever larger role within the structures of power.

e) finally, they consider that sharpening internal contradictions in each country will lead to the downfall of the democratic governments and their replacement by military regimes.

f) For this reason, the Latin American CPs must be alert to the possibility of military intervention by the U.S. in Central America, and respond to this by launching the armed struggle on a continental level.

g) In pondering the situation they feel this type of intervention is inevitable. However, if it does not occur, they will have to evaluate methods of opposition to the military governments without discarding the armed struggle when circumstances are favorable.

h) They establish support for NICARAGUA and EL SALVADOR as a priority, as well as the struggles developing in CHILE and PARAGUAY as primary goals to achieve.

i) Lastly, they indicate the need to coordinate the activities of the Latin American CPs and the

ICM in general, in order to raise their organiza-

tional level with an eye toward a global confrontation with "imperialism."

3) International Summer School and Related Activities

In the framework of this general strategy it is
fitting to mention that between November and December
1985 representatives of PRI—MONTONEROS and PRT-ERP of
ARGENTINA; MLN—TUPAMAROS, of URUGUAY; SENDERO
LUMINOSO of PERU; BRIGADA BOLIVAR, that fought in
NICARAGUA; CP, MIR and DEMOCRATIC CHILE of Chile, M—
19 of COLOMBIA, and the Argentinean CP, among others,
met in MENDOZA (ARGENTINA).

Their successive meetings, with the open participation of the Chilean CP and the support of its Argentinean counterpart, were completed with the works of
"V International Summer School" (00/15 Jan. 87).
Those meetings were also held in MENDOZA to analyze
the courses of action to follow in order to achieve
the overthrow of the government of CHILE.

The aim of this type of meetings, of different levels
of importance but multiplied throughout the continent, was the extreme left's attempt to recreate
the JCR or to create substitute organizations.

Given this, it is not surprising that in October of
1986, the Minister of the Interior of COLOMBIA said
publicly that he had indications of the creation of
an International Guerrilla Front, with the participation of M-119 from his country and Argentinean,
Chilean, Peruvian and Ecuadorian guerrillas.

Definitely, the National Guerrilla Coordination, the
immediate antecedent of this act, the operations of
American Battalion, and the coordinated actions
between the M-19 and ALFARO VIVE on the border of

COLOMBIA and ECUADOR made evident the existence of a highly consolidated regional strategy.

4) Operation Friendship

It is interesting to observe, in this brief delineation of important events, the broadness and multifaceted conformity of the ICM's strategic maneuvering.

Thus, since 1981/82 some leadership activities wee transferred from CUBA to NICARAGUA. The embassies of the latter and local organisms of "solidarity" with its regime were converted into the transmission channels for orders.

In 1985 the structure coordinating one part of the subversive activities on a continental level became known as OPERATION FRIENDSHIP. Members of the armed organizations of ARGENTINA, CHILE, COLOMBIA, BRAZIL and URUGUAY participated, as well as political and "solidarity" organizations such as the COMMITTEE IN DEFENSE OF NICARAGUA, COMMISSION OF SOLIDARITY WITH NICARAGUA, ANTI-IMPERIALIST TRIBUNAL OF AMERICA, ALL FOR THE HOMELAND MOVEMENT (linked with the PRT-ERP).

5) Conclusions

A brief consideration of the activities described until now shows that the ICM strategy in LATIN AMERICA currently is moving toward the adoption of the Sandinista model of the political-military revolutionary front. This can be seen through the following courses of action:

a) Critique of the elitist concepts that controlled the constitution of the DTBs, while continuing to support its struggle.

b) Abandonment of "narrow focus" concepts.

c) Efforts to create political fronts that bring together the greatest possible number of leftist and "independent" elements, encouraging "nationalist" sentiments under the slogans of opposition to imperialism and non-payment of the foreign debt.

d) Integration of elements of the DTBs into political fronts and capitalization of their military experience.

e) Sending of the so-called "Coffee Brigades" to Nicaragua to support the Sandinista regime and train cadres with paramilitary objectives in combat experience.

f) Creation of armed apparatuses under the cover of "Self-Defense Groups," using the most radicalized elements of partisan youth, many of them former members of coffee brigades.

g) Search for greater insertion into union structures, to exploit workers' protests with the aim of carrying out the Insurrectional Action of the Masses, and displacing traditional leadership.

h) Active participation with elements of other Latin American countries in the internal conflicts of CHILE.

i) Support of the solidarity organizations, considered as a significant and indispensable part of the revolutionary process, given their effectiveness in limiting the freedom of countersubversive action.

j) Constant action in the cultural-educational area, to generate in the population a consciousness conducive to receiving revolutionary ideology and reduce, in this way, support for the armed forces.

c. Solidarity Organizations (SO)

Without a doubt, beyond the Intelligence area, any political analyst or social investigator cannot fail to recognize the function of "Solidarity Organizations." In general, their importance in forming public opinion is recognized as well as their clear presence during and immediately after countersubversive actions. Nevertheless, we often have a vague and imprecise understanding of their origins, development and objectives. We believe it appropriate to make a very brief characterization of their structural formation and operative modalities, which we will use as a framework for our exposition. We will also illustrate their action within the Argentinean experience.

1) Characterization

Starting in 1975 and along with the development of the struggle against subversion, the first "solidarity organizations" began to appear in ARGENTINA. This terminology is take from the different conferences that, since BANDUNG (1955) constitute the subsidiary support Marxism gives to so-called "National Liberation Movements."

The immediate antecedent was the Argentina League for Human Rights, founded in 1937, as the continuation of the old International Red Aid of 1929. This organization, which functions as a front for the International Federation for the Rights of Man, decided, around 1975, to push for the creation, in our country, of Solidarity and Human Rights Commissions. They were designed to preserve the leftist cadres imprisoned during the Struggle Against Terrorism, to offer legal protection and facilitate international Marxist solidarity maneuvers, which basically followed the lines that arose from the Tricontinental of HAVANA (CUBA) in 1966.

The decision to constitute separate commissions was mostly due to the fact that the League appeared closely linked with the CP, and it was necessary to procure an adequate cover.

For its part, the DTBs, together with religious sectors infiltrated by Marxism, rounded out what can be called the "foundational" period of the SOs in the country (1975/76). New organizations were created and they came together for joint action.

Some of them, such as the Argentinean Commission for Human Rights (CADHU), had a conformation of cadres such that their direct dependence on the DTBs could not be concealed. CADHU, in particular, was a group in which members of the Montoneros, ERP, CP, Young Communist Federation, Guevarist Youth, Argentinean Socialist Party, and others participated.

The dismantling of this SO, the flight of its members, its passage to clandestinity and its redevelopment in EUROPE (SPAIN) and AMERICA (MEXICO) was only the consequence of a mistake the DTBs would not repeat. The national solidarity organizations, it was speculated, must be comprised of persons who do not, in principle, appear to be ideologically committed. Their leaders must themselves possess, or be surrounded by, an aura of personal prestige, rooted in the community so that they are protected from all risks while, at the same time, making public the "arbitrariness" of Government Power.

In this way the ICB promoted the election, for example, of outstanding persons, professionals or experts whose social position would provide them with immunity, broad dissemination of their statements and further negotiating power.

In the same way, the organizations of the Front, infiltrated organizations, pacifist movements, among others, many of which hold "consultative status" at the UN, worked together in the same way to complete a pincer maneuver from the outside, condemning the target country in international forums and determined, to some measure, its foreign support.

2) Insertion within the International Commnist Movement

At the end of World War II, the Soviet Communist Party abandoned the ideological discourse of the KOMINTERN (the CP's in the various countries occupied themselves with this), and created "front organizations" toward the end of promoting themes like "peace," "human rights," women's rights."

Their intention was to operate with structures whose make-up was not limited to committed Marxists.

In this way, the international department of the Soviet CP took charge of relations with Communist parties and leftist organizations outside of the USSR, while Department "A" of the KGB carried out "disinformation" through the front organizations, among other means.

The insertion of the national solidarity organizations within the ICM was thus achieved in two different ways. The organic form follows the following scheme:

--National Level--Front organization: Argentina Human Rights League
--International Level--Front Organizations: FIDH.
--Dependent on Department "A"--KGB

In inorganic form, the Argentinian CP, for example, stimulated--using its political weight and economic power--the creation of minor solidarity organizations, formally unconnected with the party. It also directly proceeded to infiltrate existing organizations and orient their politics toward the objectives sought after by this particular front.

In the case of the SOs directly generated by the DTBs or with large participation of their elements, the insertion is usually done through what we call "Latin American solidarity." With this they manage to connect themselves with countries such as CUBA or NICARAGUA, and extend the human rights theme in countries they are trying to destabilize.

a) Deployment

The very particular strategic worldwide deployment the ICM proposes through its fronts, SOs, infiltrated organizations, commissions and support groups, makes complete disclosure of the organism and elements involved in the maneuver almost impossible.

In our country there are around 170 SO commissions, affiliates or organizations of support,
distributed throughout the entire territory. More
than half of them are located in the FEDERAL
CAPITAL.

In the international environment some 250
organizations have been found with the previously
mentioned conditions. Some of them count with
thousands of subsidiary groups, such as AMNESTY
INTERNATIONAL (AI) in FEDERAL REPUBLIC OF GERMANY.
A territorial analysis of the origin of this
"solidarity" shows us the majority come from
WESTERN EUROPE and the AMERICAN CONTINENT and are
generated in different environments or by different types of organizations, such as those:

1) Of religious origin or participation.

2) Generated by DTBs. Normally assent is established outside the originating country.

3) Generated directly by the ICM. These are the
so-called front organizations. Their head-
quarters are usually found in Western Europe.
The most frequented capitals are GENEVA, PARIS,
HELSINKI.

4) Generated by Governmental Organizations.
Non-governmental organizations generally exist
around them, which in certain cases, have been
created or infiltrated by the ICM and enjoy
"consultive status." Their influence is sometimes significant.

b) Modes of action

The adopted modes of action are determined by the
target country's position within a particular
political juncture. Situations of injustice,

shortages, and racial discrimination are exploited, along with all damaging situations that allow for the generation of political space.

This operative makes sense within the general ICM project if we consider that passage from a military government to a constitutional one and a cessation of the Struggle Against Terrorism, mean a parallel closure, at least from a political point of view, of the cycle of individual human rights violations; that is, in the way they have been traditionally considered. Then, as the criticized situation fades in time, the solidarity organizations will face disjunction, or will maintain a message that refers exclusively to the past (and with which the public is in great part already saturated). Or they will update their message, including as human rights certain social demands (salaries, housing, labor conditions, etc.) which necessarily infers a third step that results in the transfer of this issue to the rights of one nation facing other nations, in terms commonly used and distorted by the ICM (New Economic Order, Foreign Debt, etc.). The latter are known as "third generation" rights, since they represent the right of a given population before the international community. All this allows the ICM, through the able instruments of their solidarity organizations, to gravitate freely throughout the free world.

In any event, the activity prior to taking power in a country, the destabilization of a government or the consolidation of governments affiliated with Marxism, determines the united and coordinated application of all methods: organizational, theoretical, economic and others of direct action, if necessary.

c) Coordinated action

Shortly after its creation, the national SOs created instruments of coordination and united action to improve the use of the means at their disposal.

This led to a distribution of responsibility in which, without the characteristics of subordination found in military organizations, one acted as a staff and planned the activities of them all. For example, the Center of Legal and Social Studies (CELS) of ARGENTINA functioned in this way.

Nevertheless, the SOs always reserved a considerable margin of independence that later allowed for the creation of ad hoc "coordinators" to deal with specific problems.

Because of their origins as well as their margin of independence, the national SOs maintain a fluid contact not only with their foreign counterparts but also with foundations, scientific and religious organs, etc. of their own environment, that concur with their political and economic support.

For example, in relation to the issue of financing, it is known that our country's SOs receive hidden funds, through development projects, social investigations, aid for refugees and relatives, from organizations such as: "Ford Foundation" (US), "World Council of Churches" (HOLLAND), "Twee Committee" (HOLLAND), "Brot fur die Welt" (GERMANY), "Swedish Aid for Refugees" (SWEDEN), "International Fellowship of Reconciliation" ("Brotherhood of International Reconciliation—Holland"), "Amnesty" (GREAT BRITAIN), "Catholic Organization for the Co-Financing of Development Programs" (HOLLAND), "Foundation of Norwegian

Unions" (NORWAY), "Adveniat" (GERMANY), etc.

To complete the picture of the SO situation, a list of the "PRINCIPAL ORGANIZATIONS OF SOLIDARITY WITH LATIN AMERICA" is included in the Appendix, organizations that maintain connections with the Argentinean ones.

3) Conclusions

The SOs constitute a significant part of the ICM's strategic mechanism. The former's final objectives are the ICM's partial objectives. They serve the revolutionary struggle as instruments to preserve or protect imprisoned cadres; they allow for the execution of "surface" politics that are prohibited to leftist political-military organs; they facilitate the necessary contacts for the concurrence of external forces in the maneuver, and help to create what Marxist doctrine calls "objective conditions of reality" for the development of revolutionary struggle, usually applying psychological action techniques.

Besides the specific objectives that sustain the existence of this type of organization, the nature of its operating modality and the insertion channels they open in society have increased the possibility of the Gramscian focus for taking power. In this sense, through a slow transformation of ideas, they have made viable an incipient remodeling of mentalities, which our governments must reverse.

In essence, we find the importance of the SOs in their capacity to neutralize much of the support of the popular organizations and of certain juridical-institutional resources of countries in their Struggle Against Terrorism, and to change military victories of the Liberal Forces into political defeats.

III. Civil-Military Entities Whose Activities Fall Within the ICM's Sectoral Strategy

ANTONIO GRAMSCI believed the struggle for power had to occur within a society itself, through the progressive transformation of values that sustain it. As we have been pointing out, Marxism presently feels itself most effective in a deepening of this course of action. In consequence, it knows it must operate in the cultural arena, or to speak more globally, in the arena of ideas, through which a new common sense/understanding will originate that favors and gives life to the realization of its project.

Although the psychosocial factor might be a means for strategic action, the integral nature of the ICM objective allows, above all, the operation of National Potential (NP), decomposing its sources, in other words, its beliefs, values and attitudes.

For this reason we feel it important to consider in this exposition a certain type of entity that fits, consciously, within this scheme, opens the way toward the subversion of values and tends to neutralize the institutional insertion and the specific capacities of the Military Power in the composition of National Power in each of our countries.

An entity of this type is the ORGANIZATION OF MILITARY MEN FOR DEMOCRACY, INTEGRATION AND LIBERATION OF LATIN AMERICA AND THE CARIBBEAN (OMIDELAC). Other organizations, also of civic-military nature, exist with the same or similar proposals, constituted in national precincts.

These entities operate through disinformation in the public sphere, politization and unionizing within the bosom of the armed forces themselves. When possible, they intervene in political power in decisions relating to defense, whether of a doctrinal or organic-functional nature.

Without a doubt, OMIDELAC is an archetypal organization, above all, because of the origin and orientation its founders imprinted upon it, the network of connections it establishes and the modality it uses to express its point of view.

In a brief summary we will explain its antecedents, objectives and some activities it has developed with the intent of completing, in part, the panorama that this organization and similar national ones present as a new challenge in the current situation.

a. Antecedents of OMIDELAC

The "Organization of Military Men for Democracy, Integration and Liberation of Latin America and the Caribbean," appeared in the continent only a few years ago. The first meetings date from 1982, at the initiative of exiled military men from CHILE and URUGUAY. On October 1, 1984 the First FORUM ON NATIONAL DEFENSE AND LATIN AMERICA was held in BUENOS AIRES, which can be considered the first formal step in the constitution of this entity.

Through successive meetings held in different countries, (SPAIN, CUBA, VENEZUELA, and NICARAGUA), attended by delegates from similar organizations in ARGENTINA such as the CENTER OF MILITARY MEN FOR DEMOCRACY (CEMIDA), and ARGENTINA-LATIN AMERICA UNITY (UALA), among others, the formal profile of this entity was progressively shaped.

The preparatory Commission for a "Second Forum" opportunely proposed that one central theme should be giving organic form to what wa then called

DEMOCRATIC LATIN AMERICAN AND CARIBBEAN MILITARY (MIDELAC). CHILE's National Chapter (an organization that contains military of that country oriented toward those objectives) was given the job of developing a Letter of Principles and Organic Statues for the conformation of the entity.

On April 14, 1986, during the "SECOND LATIN AMERICAN DEFENSE FORUM," also held in BUENOS AIRES, the OMIDELAC was formally constituted.

b. Objectives of OMIDELAC

From its Declaration of Principles one can deduce that the organization's principal objective is to "continue the unfinished work of liberating Latin American countries in every way from external dependence and internal domination." Therefore it calls on all military men from this part of the continent to "close ranks like one army, to obtain the demands our people need most: independence and development with peace and social justice."

To obtain these objectives it promotes and supports;

1) "The integrated and harmonious development of the Latin American and Caribbean community."

2) "The most extensive and profound Latin American and Caribbean unity and solidarity."

3) "Spiritual, doctrinal, technical and logistical union of the Latin American and Caribbean armed forces, in accordance with our loftiest ideals."

4) "The establishment of a just New International Economic Order."

5) "Non-alignment and Third World solidarity."

6) "The end of all forms of imperialism, colonialism, and neo-colonialism that affect the region."

7) "Respect for the self-determination of peoples and the principle of non-intervention."

8) "Peace and worldwide disarmament."

9) "The recuperation of control and defense of our natural resources."

10) "Social democracy with widespread participation, justice and social progress."

11) "Unrestricted respect for human rights and definite punishment for their violation."

12) "The creation of a new Security and Integrated Defense Doctrine in accordance with the interests of our people, and the establishment of a Latin American Defense System."

To concretize these aspirations the members propose:

1) "The participation of OMIDELAC on appropriate occasions in Latin America and the Caribbean—especially those concerning regional integration—proposing and promoting their postulates."

2) "The investigation, development and diffusion of projects that analyze and make proposals in the areas of National and Regional Defense in all its scope and profundity, within its own statutes."

3) "The development and implementation of all national and international initiatives that allow for the diffusion of these positions among the Armed Forces of Latin America and Caribbean, and

within society in its entirety."

c. Main Actions Developed by OMIDELAC

Some of the activities developed by this entity or similar ones are:

1) Constitution of a "National Chapter" in our country, with the participation of UAIA, CEMIDA, Latin American Institute of Strategic Studies and the Center of Ex-Combat Soldiers in the MALVINAS (Falklands).

2) In August of 1987, OMIDELAC published in BOGOTA, a book of the same name as the organization. Its origins, constitution, organization, function and objectives are explained there.

3) Between December 2 and 6, 1986, the Directive Council met in LIMA, to deal with political matters of Latin American interest, to realize academic activities and to adopt resolutions concerning the progress of the entity.

4) Between February 15 and 21, 1987 it was invited to the XI MEETING OF THE PERMANENT CONFERENCE OF POLITICAL PARTIES OF LATIN AMERICA (COPPAL), whose sessions took place in LIMA.

5) During the same year the organization had planned to hold a meeting in BRAZIL, which still has not been concretized.

6) Captain (R) RAUL VERGARA (Chilean, residing in NICARAGUA), and Captain (R) GERONIMO CARDOZO (URUGUAY), both directors of OMIDELAC, started a tour through different European countries (ITALY, FRANCE and GERMANY) to contact leaders of "European social democracy" and to solicit financial help for the activities of the entity, especially for holding an eventual Convention in

BUENOS AIRES at a date coinciding with this CONFERENCE. The coincidence of time and place of this Convention would have the object of evaluating and criticizing the resolutions adopted there.

d. Conclusions

The nuclei such as OMIDELAC and its successors are made up of retired officials who from initially different ideological positions converge, nevertheless, in actions that satisfy the ICM objective of deepening the contradictions between civil society and the armed forces. In this sense they serve, contrary to their formal and declared objectives, to neutralize institutionalized military power, as the SOs do.

If our interpretation of the Gramscian focus applied to the National Potential is accepted, we must concur that the existence of this type of organization (born precisely in circumstances in which the ICM's strategy for Latin America is modified in order to take advantage of the new institutional political alternatives generated in the Continent) can only favor the concretization of the ICM's strategic interests. Its mode of operation, the type of connections it makes, not to mention the double talk that might be seen in its objectives, announced with such a high degree of generality, confirm our viewpoint.

IV. General Conclusions

In the development of our exposition we have considered some of the ICM's modes of action in the framework of its strategic double maneuver, reflected in the environment of "International Relations" by its "Doubled-Keyboard policy."

It is interesting to point out that its entire conception of strategy is planned offensively, even when the maneuver occasionally has a defensive aim, such as the circumstances in which the SOs appeared and proliferated. This character-- which seems obvious to us, but in the light of other typical Western focuses might not be so obvious--causes them to see actions for their effectiveness in producing situations and reverting others to the benefit of its final objectives. In other words, even during a situation of retreat the ICM is promoting the conquest of power.

As we know, the ICM operative modality is flexible and integral, depending on the case in which it acts and the means available to them.

The Catholic Church has a decisive influence in LATIN AMERICA because its pastoral action is deeply rooted in the culture and history of our peoples. For this reason it also constitutes an important and legitimate factor of power, which we have examined in the first part of our work on ICM actions in what is called the "Religious Front." The application of the VATICAN II COUNCIL's recommendations about the realities and necessities of the Continent brought with it a renovation of theological reflections in the light of pastoral action. This gave way to the appearance of Liberation Theology and with it the ICM's intent to penetrate ecclesiastical structures. This attempt had some initial success in NICARAGUA and in certain Christian environments. It served, besides, the aim of backing armed struggle in some countries or giving life to the opposition movements against different regimes in the Continent.

ROME confronted this penetration action of Marxist thought through the firm pastoral action of JOHN PAUL II, the two Instructions of the Congregations for the Doctrine of the Faith and successive pronouncements of the regional and national Bishops' Conferences.

In this respect, we see that the Church has emerged strengthened from these events, to such a point that we predict that in coming years it will take even more spaces of power away from Marxist influence in the region.

The action of the "Religious Front" is a pertinent example for understanding how the ICM modified its mode of operation based on the Gramscian model in the face of the defeat of the generalization of violent struggle.

In this sense the Sandinista model of a socialist state seems a possible road for other countries of LATIN AMERICA to follow.

Concurrent with this action are the solidarity organizations, which we have analyzed as a significant piece of the ICM's strategic mechanism in the current experiences of subversion. The services they offer to the revolutionary struggle during its development or when the armed stage does not give the hoped-for results are invaluable, since they constitute the necessary mediation between clandestine elements, the popular organizations and the juridical-institutional order.

In this framework are inserted those other civil-military entities that operate at the periphery or decidedly in opposition to specific institutions. Far from promoting their declared postulates, these groups actually favor penetration and encourage discord in civil society over the true meaning of the armed forces (most especially the Army) in the shaping of the Potential of a Nation.

ACCORDS APPROVED
AT THE
XVII CONFERENCE
OF
AMERICAN ARMIES

Accords Approved
at the
XVII Conference of American Armies

Accord #4

1. THEME: Methods for combatting terrorism in America, utilizing both legal and military experience of countries worldwide who suffer it.

2. OBJECTIVE: To analyze the most adequate methods for combatting terrorism on the basis of national policy and current judicial norms, bearing in mind the permanent threat to the existence of state represented by any form of aggression by terrorist or criminal organizations which attempt to govern, or to control the government of a people or a country.

3. SCOPE: Based upon the present terrorist situation in the context of the American continent, and the continual growth of ideological penetration carried out by the International Communist Movement (ICM), to propose actions and reccomendations, fundamentally of a military and juridicial nature, to impede the latter's purposes.

4. RESOLUTION:

Whereas:

a. Terrorism is a real fact that exists in constant and periodic form in various countries of the American continent;

b. It acts by intimidating governments and societies, pursuing a variety of ends (ideological, political, etc.);

c. Existing in indiscriminate form, it affects not only the selected targets, but the whole cociety,

thus being one of the most terrible abuses of human rights;

d. This type of activity is supported and/or utilized on the continent by the ICM to destabilize governments and impose its own totalitarian ideas;

e. The above leads to the conclusion that terrorism is a common problem which affects, or will affect, directly or indirectly, the United States of America;

f. It is necessary to exchange experiences and unify criteria in relation to activity against terrorism and with regard to the possibilies of free States to confront it;

g. This threat imposes a necessity for coordinated action at every level, including the highest level of political decision-making (centralized leadership) and the employment of military power when the need for it is determined;

Therefore be it resolved;

a. That the adoption of the following measures and/or actions be proposed to the respective governments:

1) Formulate at the level of the international American community a policy against terrorism that will serve as a basis for engaging joint effective action to eliminate it;

2) Promote the establisment or improvement of specific legislation in each state, in accordance with the real nature and characteristics of terrorist acts, to increase the security of established political systems and their citizens;

3) Adopt the decision not to concede to bribery or extortion and to hold fast in the face of these actions;

4) Bring into being the coordination of intelligence activity (at the level of general and military strategy) and the opportune diffusion of information throught the appropriate systems.

b. That especially organized, equipped and trained sections or units of the Legal Forces by made available to form a front against terrorism within their respective jurisdictions.

1) Immediately distribute through SEPCA (Permanent Executive Secretaiat of the Conference of American Armies) the experiences, learnings and conclusions about terrorist acts occuring in the respective territorial jurisdictions.

Accord #5

1. THEME: International legal conventions and the conducting of non-conventional warfare.

2. OBJECTIVE: To unite efforts for conceiving a more effective international response against those who attempt to undermine our democratic traditions through acts of subversion and terrorism as methods of non-conventional warfare.

4. SCOPE:

a. Take advantages of the experiences of the American Armies to underscore the need of an international focus toward the end of elaborating effective rules of combat for struggling against terrorism and subversion.

b. Promoting the elaboration of appropriate rules of combat that recognize that the phenomenon of nonconventioanl warfare, with its aspects of terrorism and subversion, does not fit well into our present system of the law of warfare.

4.   RESOLUTION:

Whereas:

a. A growing dependence upon terrorism and subversion in an attempt to undermine the system of political, economic and military relations through which the countries of the Americas promote their national and regional interests has been noted;

b. The individual and shared experiences among the member armies in comatting this menace have thrown into relief the need for a change of our current rules of combat, fusing pragmatism and common sense with the moral vision that constitutes the essence of our democratic traditions;

Therefore be it resolved:

a. That consideration and discussion be exhorted among our armies regarding the current rules of combat relative to non-conventional warfare, taking into account practical and judicial considerations with regard to military activities of response.

b. That the Permanent Executive Secretariat be made resonsible for coordinating said discussions upon the request of any Army.   Any agreeemnt resulting from said discussions shall be subject to the approval of the Commanders of American Armies at their Conference.

Accord #6

1.   THEME: Appreciation of the situation of combined intelligence.

2. OBJECTIVE: To provide information and current intelligence on the ICM to the member countries of the Conference of American Armies.

3. SCOPE: The activity and total strategy of the ICM must be counteracted by all American countries who are objects of its aggression, who must have access to current judgements toward the end of adopting the appropriate resolutions.

4. RESOLUTION:

Whereas:

a. The ICM acts worldwide with noted political and ideological centralization, taking advantage of the weakness of the western bloc in order to destabilize democratic governments;

b. The necessary strategies for counteracting the threat represented by the ICM demand the adoption of effective actions;

c. That, for the adoption of said methods, it is necessary that the menber countries of the Conference of American Armies have access to correct and current information;

Therefore be it resolved:

a. That the appreciation of the situation of combined intelligence elaborated by the International Conference of American Armies as an instrument of information which reflects the situation and probably evolution, both in general and particularly in relation to this continent, be approved.

b. That the aforesaid appreciation of the situation of combined intelligence be sent to each one of the member countries of the Conference of American Armies for their study, analysis and/or recommendations.

Accord #10

1. THEME: Strategy of the International Communist Movement in Latin America through various modes of action.

2. OBJECTIVE: To engage in massive coordinated joint action in Latin America, based on international experience which has demonstrated that struggle carried out by each country individually is insufficient and inefective for successfully opposing the subversive and terrorist action led by the ICM.

3. SCOPE: The activity "without borders" of the ICM and its total strategy implies that a response to it must be carried out by all the American countries suffering aggression, through modes of action agreed upon and coordinated among their governments, framed in the rules of international law and of continental scope.

4. RESOLUTION:

Whereas:

a. The activity of the ICM is carried out throughout the continent without regard to borders;

b. Its strategy of penetration touches all areas of national and continental order;

Therefore be it resolved:

a. That it be recommended that the Armies deepen their studies of intelligence, of new strategies and tactics practiced by different subversive movements and by the ICM to destabilize the democracies of America.

b. That it be recommended that rapid, fluid and safe exchange of information be facilitated, permitting each country the effective realization of measures that counteract the new modes of action.

Accord #12

THEME: The value of strategic planning and combined operations in the struggle against subversion in America, maintaining the principle of non-intervention.

2. OBJECTIVE: To carry out anti-subversive operations in complete cooreperation at every level, respecting the sovereignty and self-determination of each state.

3. SCOPE:

a. The communist movement and its instruments of execution, such as subversive movements, have demonstrated activity without regard to borders; for them, international law does not exist, and this objective is to act against legally constituted democratic regimes by procuring access to political power by means of terrorist violence and other means.

b. Their action is generated by the States which create and foment the ICM, and it is executed through local subversive elements.

c. The Armies of the American States suffering subversion and terrorism historically have opposed such actions, fulfilling their respective Fundamental Charters.

d. This activity has been executed within the territory of the state suffering agression and with the participation of the army of that country.

e. The aforesaid has permitted subversives to cross the borders of neighboring countries, and to generate or augmnet subversion in the country of refuge while its borders are closed.

4. RESOLUTION:

Whereas:

a. Subversion is a real fact, and in permanent development, in American countries;

b. Its ideological inspiration is based in the International Communist Movement, a threat against the western culture existing in the American States;

c. Subversive activity is directed by the States which create and foment the ICM, without the slightest regard for international law;

d. Subversive action threatens the individual security of the States and, at the same time, the security of the hemisphere and the tranquility of its peoples

e. Its objective is to threaten democratic, legally constituted regimes, gaining access to political power by means of terrorist violence or other procedures, in order to implant totalitarian systems;

f. There are in the American Armies rules or principles of strategic, operative and tactical execution that can be jointly applied;

Therefore be it resolved:

a. That, with strict respect for the principle of non-intervention, accords be proposed among member countries of the Conference of American Armies which will allow the execution of cooperative anti-subver-

sive operations, in order to prevent subversive groups from moving from one country to another;

b. That combined planning be carried out among the member countries so resolved, sharing concepts, framework of execution and the participation of the Armies in the counter-subversive operations.

c. That emphasis be placed on courses in anti-subversive struggle, as well as strengthening existing treaties;

d. That bilateral or multilateral conferences on Intelligence and Operations be carried out, integrating specific materials for each function, so as to achieve real and effective cooperation.

Accord #14

1. THEME: Psychological operations and the communications media in the war against terrorism.

2. OBJECTIVE: To establish courses of action so that the American Armies, within the security systems of which they are a part, participate actively in reducing or nullifying the advantages obtained in the communications media in the struggle against subversion.

3. SCOPE: On the basis of the present juncture in each country, the situation generated by the presence of subversion will be evaluated, along with the support it receives, directly or indirectly, through the communications media, as a permanent threat to the security of the countries of America, with the object of unifying criteria and doctrines of the member Armies of the CEA in relation to this evidence.

4. RESOLUTION:

Whereas:

a. The sensationalism with which the communications media treat information related to terrorist acts turns terrorism into an act of propoganda, indirectly favoring the ends of subversion;

b. The advances in electronic communication frequently are taken advantage of by subversion in order to turn acts of death and destruction by terrorism into true psychological operations of the International Communist Movement;

c. The manipulation of the communications media by the legal face of subversion allows apology for subversive acts and discredits counter-subversive actions;

d. Unrestricted freedom of the communications media, established constitutionality to serve the interests of a country, is directly or indirectly taken advantage of by subversion in order to undermine the foundations of society with the clear intentions of destroying it and replacing it with another, presumably more just, one;

e. It is necessary to become aware of this psycho-social reality in order to pose actions in this area, beginning at the national level through the planning of psychological operations in support of counter-terrorism operations;

f. It is necessary to have trained personnel in order to achieve the greatest efficiency in psychological operations;

g. It is appropriate to establish effective communication for counteracting the disinformation

carried out by subversives at the international level;

h. It is important to seek a joint solution among the American Armies to the strategic efforts realized at the regional level;

Therefore be it resolved:

a. That bilateral or multilateral conferences of the American Armies be carried out in order to tighten links of cooperation, exchanging experiences in psychological operations.

b. That the Permanent Executive Secretariat of the Conference of American Armies disseminate all experiences and learnings of the member Armies on this theme that serve to help them design methodolgies appropriate to the end of counteracting the terrorist propaganda.

c. That the respective governments be advised so that they can promote information programs oriented toward counteracting subversive propaganda.

Accord #15

1. THEME: The political-strategic posture of the American Armies in the context of the CEA, in view of the need to be together in maintaining national individualities and the differences of power with the spirit of integration and continental solidarity.

2. OBJECTIVE: An adequate degree of continental security.

3. SCOPE: The American Armies believe that:

a. The ICM continues to be the common and principle threat to all American countries and, as such, must be combatted, particularly through unity and common procedures among our American Armies;

b. The security and defense of the American Continent against the ICM must consider, in addition to strictly military means, actions in the other areas of power;

c. The needs and particularities of each country should allow the Armies to participate actively in their development. In the case of such a situation, it should not be considered a permanent one.

d. It is the duty of the most developed countries to support the other American countries, as dependable allies in the struggle against the ICM, so as to create favorable conditions for constituing the American continent as a notable obstacle to the progress of Communism in the world.

RESOLUTION:

Whereas:

a. The goal of the CEA has remained unchanged over 28 years, basically concerned with the defense of the American continent against agression by the ICM;

b. The degree of security necessary in each country, and on the continent as a whole, is dependent upon the coordinated strategic actions of the four expressions of power: political, economic, psycho-social and military;

c. There exists a Panamanian consciousness that is necessary to strengthen the integration and spirit of continental solidarity;

d. The American Armies, in function of their affinities, can make a specific contribution to a greater and more effective approximation among the countries of the continent;

e. The CEA is, without any doubt, a priveleged forum for deepening the study and debate, taking into account that it offers a qualitative contribution to the road to relative solutions to the security of the

American continent, which the vision of this issue requires.

Therefore be it resolved:

a. That it be considered necessary and convenient to deepen studies which allow establishing the political-strategic posture of the American Armies in view of the need to come together in maintaining national individualities and differences of power, with the spirit of integration and continental solidarity in view, in the final analysis, of an adeqaute degree of security for the American continent, with the dimension the situation requires, coordinating these actions in the overall framework of the areas of power: political, economic, psychosocial and military;

b. That each American Army be required to carry out these studies within the situational, institutional and legal frameowrk of its respective country, and later inform the CEA.

c. That, given the fundamental importance of the theme, the CEA can be required to assign priority to the theme in its treatment and dissemination.

KEEPING CONTROL
OVER LATIN AMERICA

THE TWO
STRATEGIC DOCUMENTS
OF THE
SANTA FE COMMITTEE

Keeping Control
Over Latin America

The Two Strategic Documents
of the Santa Fe Committee

The secret documents of the Intelligence
Conference of American Armies (CIEA) aim to present a
strategy for the continued, common control of Latin
America. This strategy has not come out of nowhere,
however; it is the product of earlier "national
security" doctrines and is a way of assimilating the
strategy discussion in the United States. And
although this latter discussion has often been
inconsistent, its main foci are easily identifiable.
One highlight was the "Santa Fe Paper" of 1980,
representing an important point of departure for
Reagan's Latin American Policy.

The Council for Inter-American Security in
Washington has always been a strictly rightwing-
oriented, private organization, involving conservative academics, ex-military officers and other
interested persons desiring to formulate Latin
American policy in the light of Reaganism. Its
"Santa Fe Committee" was, in 1980, in the frontline
of those presenting the upcoming Reagan administration with a straightforward anti-communist approach
to Latin American policy.

In 1988 the same authors drafted "Santa Fe
II," which continued the line of the first document,
while changing the emphasis slightly in order to be
acceptable to the future Bush government. Both Santa
Fe papers derive from a close substantive and strategic connection with the secret documents of the CIEA.
They have similar goals and ideological premises, and
produce similar results and proposals. It is generally asserted that they are secret documents but they
are not: their purpose is to have an impact on poli-

tical debate about Latin American policy in the United States. So they may be freely obtained by members of the public, while remaining of major significance. The Santa Fe documents of 1980 and 1988 may be ordered from: Council for Inter-American Security, Inc., 305 Fourth St., N.E., Washington, D.C. 20002.

The First Santa Fe Paper

The first Santa Fe paper bore the name "A New Inter-American Policy for the Eighties." It was primarily directed against the policy of President Carter, which was considered to be "weak" and sought to launch a new Latin American policy with great ideological panache.

The starting point was geopolitical. Latin America was said to be indispensable to the US superpower role, with the Soviet Union in the process (through regional "proxies") of politically undermining Latin America and bringing it under military control - as part of its plan of global conquest.

"Even the Caribbean, America's maritime crossroad and petroleum refining center, is becoming a Marxist-Leninist lake. Never before has the republic been in such jeopardy from its exposed southern flank. Never before has American foreign policy abused, abandoned and betrayed its allies to the south in Latin America. It is time to take the initiative. An integrated global foreign policy is essential. It is time to sound a clarion call for freedom, dignity and national self interest which will echo the spirit of the American people. Either a Pax Sovietica or a worldwide counter-projection of American power is in the offing. The hour of decision can no longer be postponed" (Santa Fe I, p.2).

The Soviet Union was said to be cutting the West off from its energy (chiefly oil) and other resource supplies, and hemming it in, as with the People's Republic of China. It already had been very successful in the Middle East, the Indian Ocean, southern Africa and was set to "Finlandise" Western Europe and alienate Japan from the United States.

The paper claimed that the United States must concentrate on Latin America and the Caribbean: "The Caribbean rim and basin are spotted with Soviet surrogates and ringed with socialist states." These included Cuba, Nicaragua, Grenada and also Guyana and Jamaica. The stability and security of other countries in the region (notably El Salavador and Guatemala) was likewise extremely doubtful. Nicaragua and Cuba were Soviet proxies and satellites and thus were particularly responsible for the export of terrorism and revolution to their neighbors.

Against this background, characterized by a sense of urgency and even alarmism, proposals were then made, in different areas, as to how the US might then hang onto Latin America as part of its power base. The military part, which was deliberately dealt with first, made mention of the revival of the Rio Pact and the Inter-American Defense Council, the initiation of more regional security agreements and the revival and reinforcement of US military aid for the Latin American armed forces.

A special chapter was devoted to "internal subversion" in Latin American countries. Reference was made to the "integral link between internal subversion and external aggression": "Given the Communist commitment to utilize every available means to overthrow the capitalist order and to transform the world, internal and external security become inseparable" (Santa Fe I, p.17). Here we also find one of the basic concepts of low intensity conflict (LIC) which was to resurface in the documents of the CIEA.

It is interesting in this context to see what importance the Santa Fe paper gave to the ideological conflict, which is under constant scrutiny in a whole series of proposals at different points. For example. it urged that US policy on Latin America should "insulate itself" from the general and specialized media, said to engage in propaganda for hostile forces.

President Carter's human rights policy had to be dropped, the paper said, and replaced by a "policy of political and ethical realism". The US government should work "through and with" the AFL-CIO in order to tackle statism and centralism in Latin America.

The paper was particularly negative about the Theology of Liberation. "U.S. foreign policy must begin to counter (not react against) liberation theology as it is utilized in Latin America by the 'liberation theology' clergy. The role of the church in Latin America is vital to the concept of political freedom. Unfortunately the Marxist-Leninist forces have utilized the church as a political weapon against private property and productive capitalism by infiltrating the religious community with ideas less Christian than Communist" (Santa Fe I, p.20).

In a section on education as a political tool, the authors stated clearly:

"The United States must seize the ideological initiative. (...) Education must instill the idealism that will serve as an instrument for survival. The war is for the minds of mankind. Ideo-politics will prevail. (...) Thus, whoever controls the educational system determines the past – or how it is viewed – as well as the future. Tomorrow is in the hands and heads of those who are being taught today. (...) We should export ideas and images which will encourage individual liberty, political responsibility and respect for private property. A campaign to capture the Ibero-American intellectual elite through the media of radio, television, books, articles and pamphlets, plus grants, fellowships and prizes must be initiated" (Santa Fe I, p.32).

Besides military and ideological proposals, Santa Fe I particularly stressed the economic sector. Energy policy (including the promotion of domestic uses of nuclear energy), technology transfer (to be markedly liberalized), agriculture (with suggestions of specializing Latin American production and improving access to the US market), the Latin American debt and economic, trade and investment policy (with the proposal to abolish Latin American capital markets, closer regional cooperation and the creation of a Latin American monetary fund) - all these were additional emphases, backed up by ideas on specific points and economic sectors.

The Santa Fe paper of 1980 concluded by stressing that three countries of the hemisphere were of particular strategic importance to the United States: Brazil, Mexico and Cuba. Brazil was considered the key country in South America. There has been no criticism at all of its human rights record and, instead, intensive cooperation in the field of technology and, in particular, nuclear energy.

Mexico is of particular importance to the Unites States, if only due to its proximity, the millions of legal and illegal immigrants, and its oil and gas reserves - not to speak of its political influence in Central America. Close cooperation in these fields was regarded as essential.

The Santa Fe committee tackled Cuba with considerable ideological zeal. "The United States can no longer accept the status of Cuba as a Soviet vassal state. Cuban subversion must be clearly labelled as such and resisted. The price Havana must pay for such activities cannot be a small one. The United States can only restore its credibility by taking immediate action. The first steps must be frankly punitive" (Santa Fe I, p.45). As one possible means of doing so, the paper proposed opening an anti-Cuban radio station, and continued with its customary frankness, "If propaganda fails, a war of national liberation against Castro must be launched."

In all, Santa Fe I offered a synthesis of offensive ideological crusader mentality against a "Soviet-Cuban-Nicaraguan axis," with a package of pragmatic economic and political measures. It actually sought to present an integrated general outline of a Latin American policy designed exclusively to serve US power interests and contribute to a global power struggle against the Soviet Union and "communism" - without any moral doubts at all. It is horrifying to see the militance and unscrupulousness with which it presented its own proposals: The Third World War is already being waged and one must respond accordingly. In any case, war, not peace, is the normal state of affairs. "Certainly, in war there is no substitute for victory; and the United States s engaged in World War III. (...) Containment of the Soviet Union is not enough. (...) America must take the lead. For not only are U.S.-Latin American relations endangered, but the very survival of this republic are at stake" (p.53).

The authors premised their ideas on an all-out war with the Soviet Union, albeit of "low intensity". All available means could serve to reach the victory - military aggression, military and economic aid, ideological struggle and economic reforms. It was not a defensive matter, but aimed at the offensive victory of US controlled capitalism in all countries of the continent of America.

Santa Fe II

In 1988 the Santa Fe Committee of the Council for Inter-American Security came up with a new paper. This time it was entitled "Santa Fe II – A Strategy for Latin America in the '90s." Even though this document rightly placed itself in the tradition of the preceding one, it is considerably different in character.

The beginning was familiar. "The Americas are still under attack. We warned of this danger in 1980. The attack is manifested in communist subversion, terrorism and narcotics trafficking."

It continued in this style: a "communist network of subversion and terror" aims at defeating the (military) forces of the US in Latin America and thus limiting their room for manoeuvre in Europe and elsewhere. The "subversive-terrorist threat" has not abated in the last decade – on the contrary, it has grown.

Compared with the original Santa Fe paper, Santa Fe II is remarkably brief at these points: it uses somewhat stereotypical terms and sounds as though it is reciting a ritual.

The substance and major part of the text is concerned upon developing the bases of a long term Latin American policy. These ideas center on the question of the "democratization" of Latin America. This may appear amazing at first sight, seeing that the Santa Fe Committee has become known that as the advocate of control by power politics, and not as a defender of democratic participation. However, on closer inspection the connection becomes clear. Regarding the long-term stabilization of Latin America in the American-Western sense, not only are military dictatorships inadequate for this, but also are forms of governments based on purely formal electoral mechanisms. Long-term stability can only be achieved, it is thought, when a political culture has been established that has totally absorbed western-democratic values; it is not just a case of a traditional authoritarian "regime," and not just formal democratic mechanisms, which can be given up too easily.

Yet what is the essence of this "democratic regime"? It is by no means a matter of demanding democratic participation for the population (majority), or similar ideas geared to the interests of the population. The point is rather to integrate liberal economic views with strategies of a regimented democracy.

The "democracy" of Santa Fe II is a counter-model to socialist models, and also to state regulated bourgeois societies. "The dirigiste regime increasingly substitutes itself for the initiative of the citizen and steadily reduces the autonomous sphere of civil society" (Sante Fe II, p.6).

Even where Latin American tradition is not socialist, it is increasingly characterized by an interventionist and obstructive state machinery, which hinders economic development (statism). "Administrations may be unstable and change, but all tend to call for the expansion of the role of the regime during their time" (Santa Fe II, p.6).

The "democratic" counter model of Santa Fe II makes the unleashing of the free market the centerpiece of the "democratic regime", claiming that democracy means individual freedom and equating individual freedom with free enterprise. "The democratic regime is one where it is the responsibility of government to preserve an existing society from external attack or encroachment by the state apparatus" (p. 7).

In this context, "drug-traffickers, terrorists and an expansive state" are regarded as threatening as an extension of "the imperial tyranny of the Soviets." The US "cannot stand by and watch the escape from poverty be undercut by" "economic policies which destroy the country" (p. 8). Santa Fe II states that "The trends toward centralized control of economic activity and the blurring of the distinction between society and the regime" are statist and integrally nationalist. Even if elected officials and governments took such views thew "anti-democratic regime" would not yet be overcome. Elections then would not help much.

Democratization means primarily denationalization. The introduction of such a "democratic model" will not be acceptable to all parts of the population, so that organized resistance is to be expected. Here the paper has a solution ready. "The U.S. should recognize the need of governments attempting to create regimes to restrain anti-democratic parties" (p. 11). This uninhibited statement is only comprehensible in the context of the concept of democracy outlined above: organizations opposing the liberal economic views of the paper would be virtually "anti-democratic" and it would thus be legitimate to limit their political room to maneuver. That is not exactly what is generally understood by democracy at work!

The centerpiece of the democratization program of Santa Fe II is the privatization of semi-state ventures, denationalization of decision making process and economic deregulation, along with "democratic capitalism," defined as "free enterprise systems and national capital markets" (p.15).

Santa Fe does not devote a separate chapter to "internal subversion." Instead it deals more intensively and systematically with the question of cultural hegemony, explicitly resorting to Gramsci (p.10; see also note 40 of Introduction to this volume).

The authors apparently assume that the threats to American interests is now more strongly derived from ideological and cultural policy than from military assaults or open uprisings. For this reason, more detailed proposals are made as to how the US can ideologically take the initiative. In the tradition of Santa Fe I, the ideological and cultural conflict is envisioned as a kind of "war."

Santa Fe II states that liberation theology "is a political doctrine disguised as religious belief having an anti-Papel and anti-free enterprise meaning in order to weaken society's independence from statist control. (...) We see the innovation of Marxist doctrine grafted onto a long running cultural and religious phenomenon. The attack is not targeted at only one or two components of the culture. It is effective over a broad front that seeks to redefine all of the culture in new terminology, so that just as Catholicism is redefined by liberation theologians, so art is transformed, books are reinterpreted, curricula are overhauled. The thrust of cultural penetration in Latin America is followed by the various Marxist educational theorists in the schools and universities. State control over education is increasing through textbooks and manuals and more is mandated by education bureaucracies. (...) The ascendency of the left in much of the mass media throughout Latin America must be understood also in this context. No democratic election can change the continuing shift toward the statist regime if the "consciosness-raising industry" is in the hands of the statist intellectuals. The mass media, the churches and the schools will continue to shift democratic reforms towards statism if the U.S. and fledgling democratic governments do not recognize this is a regime struggle" (p.11).

Here an old motive arises again. And the struggle is again one between good and evil, although the
thrust of the argument in Santa Fe II is now against
dirigism in general and socialism is only understood
as one of its (albeit particularly unpleasant) forms.
And this struggle is now seen as an ideological
conflict as well, no longer primarily as a military
and subversive threat. But this struggle for a self-
defined democracy is also to be waged with great
determination. Political forces opposing the
development of democratization should be "minimized
as much as possible".

Santa Fe makes concrete proposals about waging
the ideological war. First it stresses the importance of International Military Education and
Training (IMET), that directly teaches "democratic
values," besides military skills. In no way must it
be coupled with the repayment or non-repayment of aid
loans, as the US would thus deprive itself of an
important means of influence.

Secondly, it recommends the massive strengthening
of the role of the United States Information Agency
(USIA). This body has the task of opposing the
cultural offensive of the left a la Gramsci. "The
USIA is our agency for fighting the cultural war"
(p.13). Thee proposals are supplemented by the
authors' proposal to operate a selective human rights
policy. On the one hand, the legal systems in the
region should be fostered and, on the other, a
distinction must be made between human rights organizations that support a "democratic regime" and those
promoting Gramsci-style state dirigism.

The second Santa Fe paper, like its predecessor,
deals with Mexico, Brazil and Cuba in particular
detail. In addition to the countries mentioned, the
new paper now turns to Panama and Columbia, with
particular focus on the latter.

Nicaragua also gets a mention, typically in a chapter called "Low Intensity Conflict." It is argues that "containing" Nicaragua would be costly and in the long-term ineffective. Hence the goal must consist in "democratizing" the country. Interestingly, in this context there is less reference to military instruments then, again, to influencing public opinion and the media.

The sanctions on Cuba are notable in Santa Fe II. They are much more cautious than the wording used in Santa Fe I. Instead of calling for a "war of liberation" against Cuba, the stress is now on the "period after Castro," who – it is said – cannot stay in office much longer if only for reasons of age. The goal of a "political reorientation of Cuba" is not abandoned, but the degree of aggressiveness is somewhat reduced.

Now there is talk of "high-level talks with the Soviet Union" in order to attain the withdrawal of troops from the island. Then talks should be opened "with Castro or his successor". The United States should beam more radio and TV programs to Cuba "as a means of civic education for creating a democratic regime" (p.31).

The goal is still to make Cuba into a "free and independent member of the international community" – in other words, to topple the socialist regime there – but there is less verbal muscle flexing. At the end of the '90s, the Santa Fe Committee has nothing more to offer than, "With the very real possibility that Castro will retire some time in the '90, U.S. policy makers must be aware that a regime crisis is in the making" (p.33).

The Importance of the Two Santa Fe Papers

The two papers were written by the same group of authors and are based on the same political ideology.

They are rooted in massive anti-communism and subordinate everything to the goal of US control of Latin America, considered necessary for geopolitical reasons. In spite of this identical starting point, the two papers are not identical in political substance and wording; they differ in political assessment and emphasis.

There are three principle reasons for this: first, the mixed experiences with Reagan's Latin America policy; second, the altered political and economic parameters for US policy in Latin America and, third, shifts in political emphasis from Reagan to Bush.

Reagan's policy toward the western hemisphere, in particular Central America, presents a contradictory picture. Any assessment naturally depends on the criteria applied and there are a variety to offer. If you start from the goals formulated by the Reagan Administration and its closest forces - e.g. the Santa Fe Committee - at the beginning of its term, then the results were unimpressive. They never managed to smash the FMLN guerilla movement in El Salvador through a military, political and economic appeasement policy (thought to be feasible in less than a year). Even the political stability of El Salvador, apparently achieved around 1986 through the project of a Christian-Democratic backed democratization of the country as devised by Santa Fe - must be considered a failure now, at the beginning of the nineties.

The aim in Nicaragua was, from the beginning, "to get rid of the Sandinistas," i.e. to oust them and reverse the revolution. The Reagan Administration had imposed trade boycotts to this end, tried diplomatic isolation, launched an immense propaganda campaign - the focus of its policy - created the contras, then financing, training and arming them.

Despite these great efforts the Sandinistas were not brought down, which the head of the Latin American Department in the State Department, Eliot Abrams, deplored as late as February 1989, blaming it on the Reagan government's lack of determination.

At the same time there were growing signs of a creeping destabilization of Honduras and Costa Rica, hitherto seemingly so stabile, and it was remarkable that the brutal and successful counter-insurgency campaign of the Guatemalan military in the early '60s was achieved almost without US military aid. The tough line taken in 1981 against Cuba - with great verbal rhetoric - proved unfeasible and was quietly dropped after the resignation of Secretary of State Alexander Haig. Finally, it should be pointed out that during its second term the Reagan Administration gradually lost the ability totally to dictate its policy to the small Central American states. While it had been easily possible to apply pressure on the Contadora process during the first term, causing it to fail, this was no longer possible with the Arias plan the second time around.

However, it would be too simple to regard Reagan's Central American and South American policy as a failure. After all his administration had succeeded if not in defeating, at least in keeping the FMLN in El Salvador out of power, which they had seemed to be nearing in the period from 1981 to 1983. As for Nicaragua, while not bringing down the FSLN, the US government did manage to enforce a toughening of domestic policy, a militarization of the society and the wrecking of Nicaragua's economy. In 1979 - 80 Nicaragua had been a model of an anti-dictatorial revolution in Latin America - at the end of Reagan's term of office there was no longer any question of this.

The cheap success of the Reagan administration through the conquest of the tiny Caribbean island of

Grenada in October, 1983, was substantially second-rate, but inestimable in terms of political psychology, even in the United States.

The Santa Fe Committee drew its conclusions from this mixed balance sheet. The excessive fixation of the Reagan Administration on Central America was to be disrupted and the important countries of South America and Mexico focussed on more clearly. The problems of "military subversion" had, from the US perspective, proved less central than the political and economic questions of Latin America, which appeared at least equally dangerous to stabilization in the medium term.

This rethinking of its own position corresponded to a change in the parameters of United States politics. In the early '80s all observers had concentrated their attention on the Central American flashpoint, and the Santa Fe Committee and the Reagan administration had feared an expansion of the revolutionary wave to Panama and Mexico. From the mid '80s, however, other issues occupied center stage, notably the gradual replacement of traditional military dictatorships in South and Central America by civilian governments. Brazil, Argentina, Uruguay and Guatemala were the most important cases. However, these and similar questions were also on the agenda in Haiti, Chile, Paraguay and Panama. The future of the PRI government in Mexico is also of considerably higher significance to the US then events in tiny Caribbean states. In these questions the US administration did not have cut-and-dried policies for the effective defense of US interests. It was thus hardly surprising that the santa Fe Committee was particularly concerned with the questions of "democratizing" Latin America.

Finally, the change in government from Reagan to Bush had obvious effects on the wording of the second paper. Reagan had been extremely ideologically committed regarding Central America, developing – with some of his staff – a downright crusader mentality against Nicaragua; Bush and his team – even when they tactically chose to continue the Reagan line – were expected to be more pragmatic. Even though Bush would not pursue a "liberal" Central and South American policy, there would be less ideological fire. And if the Santa Fe Committee wanted to influence the new government, it had to take appropriate account of this in wording its proposals.

If we take the two Santa Fe documents together and relate them to the secret documents of the CIEA, we are struck by the many parallels and common positions. It would be wrong, however, to seek to attribute this to a cause–and–effect relationship, as though the Conference of the American Armies had copied parts of the Santa Fe I paper, or Santa Fe II had plagiarized part of the CIEA papers. In reality the similarities can be explained by the fact that both sets of papers were drawn from the same political and ideological source: from the political and military debate conducted chiefly in the United States on low intensity warfare and the control of the Third World. This is a discussion that is being internationalized through close contact between US and Latin American military and also through events like the annual Conference of the American Armies.

EPILOGUE

THE 1990s:
A HOPE FOR THE THIRD WORLD

The 1990s:
A Hope for the Third World

I dedicate this theological reflection to our six Jesuit brothers murdered in El Salvador—the first conscious and planned attempt against a team of Theologians of Liberation.

The world changed abruptly in the last months of 1989. Events in the socialist countries of eastern Europe, the process of **perestroika** in the USSR, the war in El Salvador (with tragic aggression against the people and the massacre of the six Jesuit priests), the end of the Pinochet dictatorship in Chile, the popular advance of Lula in Brazil, and, finally the arrogant aggression of the imperialist power against the nation of Panama. We could add many other important events in Haiti, Colombia, South Africa, the Middle East, India, the Philippines, etc.

Within a few months, the world changed—we now have another world. But has the life and death situation of the poor and oppressed masses of the Third World really changed? The Berlin Wall fell, and the rich world trembled with joy. In reality, the fall of the wall was very positive. But we are aware that another gigantic wall is being constructed in the Third World, to hide the reality of the poor majorities. A wall between the rich and the poor is being built, so that poverty does not annoy the powerful and the poor are obliged to die in the silence of history. A wall of silence is being built so that the rich world forgets the Third World. A wall of disinformation, or of bad information, is being built to casually pervert the reality of the Third World.

El Salvador: On November 1, the army savagely murdered 11 of the most important leaders of the popular movement. On November 16, the same army murdered six Jesuit priests along with two household servants. Many people, horrified, condemned these crimes, but very few have reflected upon the meaning of these deaths. In fact, they condemned the crime while simultaneously giving political support to the president of El Salvador. The six priests formed a team that reflected, taught, wrote from within the process of liberation of the Salvadoran people. They were friends, they prayed together, they thought together about the future of the people, they created pastoral strategies and policies of liberation. In the strict sense of the word, they were a team which practiced the Theology of Liberation on a day to day basis. The death of the Jesuits was a terrorist act against the Theology of Liberation. They were killed precisely because they did liberating theology in a concrete process of popular liberation. Witnesses told us that, after murdering these priests, they took out their brains—they "de-brained" them, to be very sure that their intelligence was really dead. Within this team, too much holiness and intelligence had been accumulated and that had become unbearable to the powerful. With the death of the Jesuits and of the Theology of Liberation, an effort is made to take from the poor their voice, their hope, their awareness, their faith, their spiritual power.

The most important process of the last decade in Central America, and possibly in all the Third World, is the power and importance acquired by popular social movements: movements of solidarity, human rights movements, women's liberation movements, alternative health care movements, ecological movements, indigenous and Afro-American movements, cultural and artistic movements, literacy movements, popular education and alternative communication movements, Christian base movements, labor movements, cooperativist movements for alternative production and commercialization, etc., etc. The whole people is putting itself in motion for life, for health, for culture, for dignity, for liberty. These popular social movements are not directly seeking to take political power, they are seeking radically to transform civil society. They seek to create a new popular social consensus, which integrates all senses of life: economic, social, political, cultural, ethical and spiritual. The social movements create a new popular identity, where all social identities are brought out: peasant, worker, indigenous, Afro-American, women's identity, national, cultural and religious identity. The people are getting in motion, and are identifying themselves as the subject of their own history.

These popular social movements comprise, in many countries a significant and powerful popular majority which radically questions the dominant system and seeks to reconstruct a new power ad a new society based upon the identity and power of the people themselves. The people first take power in civil society, creating a popular consensus that is alternative to the system of domination. From this base, the type of political power necessary for a global transformation of society is discussed and effectively constructed. In these popular social movements lie the greatest power and wealth of the Third World.

Within these popular social movements, the Ecclesial Base Communities (CEBs) were born, which, in Latin America, continue to be one of the most important phenomena, both in the social and theological arenas. The CEBs represent the possibility of the poor majorities to participate creatively, with their own consciousness and culture, in the church. The CEBs also represent the possibility for the church to be present, with its own identity and force, in the midst of the popular social movements. Through the CEBs, the poor and oppressed people participate creatively in the church, and also through the CEBs the church participates evangelically in the popular social movements. The CEBs create within the popular movement an ethical, spiritual and transcendent force, which dynamizes the march of the people and with which the people feel identified. Both the popular social movements and the Ecclesial Base Communities within them provide us with an historical key for understanding the Third World and its possible future of liberation and life. Herein lies our force as the Third World. The Third World is poor in money, technology and arms, but its wealth lies in the people, especially when that people rescue their humanity and cultural and religious identity through social movements.

The National Security Doctrine and all counterinsurgency programs presently basically are seeking to destroy the popular social movements and the CEBs that are within them. The political, and political-military, movements and guerilla groups, who seek to take political power, are dangerous for the system, but to the degree that they isolate themselves from the popular movements, they can be destroyed. These political movements are powerful and meaningful only when they are born and grow within the popular social movements and are capable of representing or identifying with such a popular movement, never separating from it. The popular social movements are the base and force of the political movements of liberation. At present, repression and war are directed fundamentally against popular social movements, against alternative social movements, against grassroots movements. The system cannot easily isolate and destroy these movements, especially when they are massive and significant, and when they have adequate political expression. The insertion of popular political groups into popular social movements has allowed political groups to find a broad social base, and also has allowed poor and oppressed people to increase their force quantitatively and qualitatively. Sterile and destructive elitism and vanguardism are overcome in this way, and we discover the political, cultural and spiritual force of a people on the move, or the popular movement. This has been the great political learning of the 1980s, and it allows us to confront the new decade with strength and optimism.

The system cannot tolerate Christians making their faith active and aware within the popular movements, nor that the church is reconstructed within these popular movements. The CEBs and the model of church called the Church of the Poor, which is born from the CEBs, is the space where the presence and privileged revelation of God among the world of the poor and in the popular movements is manifested. The Theology of Liberation reflects, critically and systematically, on this presence and revelation of God among the poor and oppressed. For this very reason, implacable repression is unleashed against the CEBs, against the Church of the Poor, against the Theology of Liberation. This is why, in El Salvador, the popular leaders were murdered first, then the six Jesuits who did Theology of Liberation within the popular movement. The Theology of Liberation is that which best expresses and empowers the spiritual and religious force of the Latin American people; it is the theology that is creating a spiritual vision on the basis of the political and cultural reality of the Third World. It is the theology that is allowing us to think about Christianity from the reverse side of history and against western neocolonial Christianity. The contribution of the Theology of Liberation, with all its cultural and ecumenical pluralism, to the integral liberation of the Third World, is another of the great lessons of the 1980s, and against which the political and military leaders of the rich world already are reacting. (See the Santa Fe I and Santa Fe II declarations.)

In this context, the movement for neoconservative restoration within the Catholic hierarchy, and the Protestant fundamentalist religious movements, are very worrisome. These movements respond to the same repressive logic of the dominant system against the popular social movements, especially against the spiritual liberation dimension which becomes meaningful within them. The Salvadoran military murdered the six Jesuits with impunity; but are not all those who condemn the Theology of Liberation, satanizing it and calling it "Marxist" and "communist," equally responsible? It is incredible how some sectors of the Catholic hierarchy have internalized military authoritarianism and the National Security Doctrine. Just as the military identify the nation with the state, so these bishops identify the people of god with the hierarchy. If, for the military, there can be no political opposition since they see all opposers as enemies, likewise many bishops see all dissidents as heretics and enemies of the church. For both the military and for certain restorationist bishops, human rights do not exist for those who criticize the institution. The institution is the Truth, and those who are opposed to the Truth have no rights. There is no democracy for the "enemies of democracy." There is no Canon Law for the "enemies of Canon Law." Obedience is required because one has the power to impose it.

If military authoritarianism is terrible, this ecclesiastical authoritarianism now being imposed within the restorationist Catholic Church is much worse. The ideological authoritarianism of the fundamentalists is likewise unbearable. The restorationist neoconservative movement dangerously identifies the church with the authoritarian and dogmatic currents of the centers of power. Catholic restoration and Protestant fundamentalism are transforming the Christian churches into Churches of Power. They are once again becoming a great Western Neocolonial Christendom, whose center is Europe and whose absence, forgotten and despised, is the church born of the cultural and spiritual richness of the Third World. As one theologian said, "The church can no longer transform the world, because the world already has transformed the church." In the 1990s, we shall have to organized an evangelizing mission from the Third World to the rich world that is lost in consumerism, materialism, drugs and idolatry.

Europe changed in November of 1989, but some changes that perhaps are positive for Europe can mean reinforcing the mechanisms of domination for the Third World. The Berlin Wall fell, but simultaneously, the civilian population of El Salvador was bombed and a team of six Jesuit priests was murdered. Further, the changes in the rich world of the north are being used to delegitimize the popular struggles of the peoples of the Third World. Certainly there is a positive liberation process in the rigid structure and ideologies of the socialist societies of eastern Europe, but the delegitimation of the Third World popular movements does not follow. Many are trimphasistically proclaiming the death of "communism," hiding the force of liberation that has surged up out of the root of the popular socialist movements; above all, the popular social movements of the Third World are hidden. To the degree that the east-west contradiction disappears, the north-south contradiction, that between the centers of power in the industrialized countries and the poor Third World countries, grows. The north-south contradiction will be the contradiction of the '90s.

In this the decade of the '90s, we shall have to be more faithful that ever to defend life or the poorest and most oppressed. Very soon, 80 percent of humanity will live in the Third World, and life here is seriously threatened. To defend the life of the poor of the Third World is the imperative of humanity, but, above all, the imperative of the Third World church and especially of the Theology of Liberation. The bombing of poor civilian neighborhoods of El Salvador and the murder of the six Jesuits are acts that can rapidly be extended to the whole Third

World. The powerful are disposed to bomb, if necessary, all the poor peoples of the earth, and to
murder all the thinkers and theologians of liberation. If, in the Third World, the popular social
movements and Ecclesial Base Communities continue to
be strengthened, the powerful will try to kill all of
them. The Third World peoples are already being
killed with an immoral demand for payment of the
external debt, with militarism, with consumerism,
with the obligatory production of drugs, with imposed
cultural barbarism, with religious sects, etc. But,
if necessary, they can escalate to bombs, to terrorism and to massacres; the powerful will not
hesitate to do it (as they already are doing in El
Salvador, Guatemala, Panama, Colombia, etc.). And
the campaign against the theology of Liberation and
the CEBs, being carried out by the neoconservative
restoration movement in the Catholic Church, also
seeks to destroy the popular subject in the church,
and is complicit in the same logic of death against
the Third World poor. The 1990s, then, will be the
decade of the defense of life for the poor majorities
of the Third World, both in society and church, with
political and cultural arms as well as spiritual and
theological arms.

The advance of the popular forces in Brazil is also
a fact that is changing the world. Perhaps it is an
even more significant fact than the events in eastern
Europe. The advance of the popular forces in Brazil
is a triumph of social movements, the triumph of
labor movements, of peasant and indigenous movements,
of women's and youth movements, of alternative
culture and health care movements. It is also the
triumph—why not say so?--of the Ecclesial Base Communities and of the Theology of Liberation, to the
degree that these animate the march of the people
toward their full and total liberation.

In this context, we must remain faithful in defense
of the threatened life of the poor; we must remain

faithful to the presence of the revelation of God among the poor of the Third World; we must continue to be faithful and persevere with the Theology of Liberation and the Ecclesial Base Communities. While the people struggle for life and justice, and while we maintain our faith and hope in the God of life, we shall continue to do Theology of Liberation, whether the powerful and the Catholic restorationists like it or not.

The world has certainly changed in the last months, but these changes must not hide the reality of the Third World. The structures of power, both political and religious, can change but, for use, the most important thing is that the people begin to move ahead–that the poor majorities of the Third World begin to awaken, to become conscious of themselves, and to develop a culture and religion of liberation. The popular social movements are born, power is taken by the grassroots. The blood of the six Jesuit martyrs of El Salvador, and the anonymous blood of the whole people, will be transformed in the Resurrection, in the Realm of God, into new heaven and earth, the New City, new men and women here and now in the Third World.

Pablo Richard
Central America
December 20, 1989

The Most Important Solidarity Organizations in Latin America

1. ALDHU Latin American Association for Human Rights

2. AAJ American Association of Jurists

3. ALADDR Latin American Association of Lawyer for the Defense of Human Rights

4. CEETM Center for Scientific Studies of the Third World

5. CODESPA Committe of Denunciation and Solidarity with the Argentine People

6. CBSFPDA Brazilian Committee of Solidaritty for the Families of the Detained-Disappeared in Argentina

7. CAS   Argentine Solidarity Committee

8. CSPSRD South American Committee for Peace, Regional Security and Democracy

9. CSDPA Solidarity Committee for Paraguayans Disappeared in Argentina

10. COSLUPAD Committee in Solidarity with the Struggle of the Argentina People for Democracy

11. CESPA Ecuadorian Committee for Solidarity with the Argentinian People

12. COSPA Committe in Solidarity with the People of Argentina

13. CSL Latin American Solidarity Committee

14. CBS-ES Brazilian Committee in Solidarity with Latin American Peoples- "Holy Spirit"

15. CSPAC Committee in Solidarity with the People of Central America

16. COSOFAM Committee for Solidarity with the Families of the Detained, Executed and Disappeared in Argentina

17. CLAI Latin American Council Church

18. CLAIP Latin American Christian Peace Conference

19. CAE Argentine Christians in Exile

20. CAL Latin American Coordinating Committee

21. CLAMOR The Peals of the Miserable, the Wretched, the Dying

22. FUDA The Families and Relatives in Argentina of the Disappeared Uruguayans

23. FPDDA The Families and Relatives in Argentina of the Disappeared and Detained Paraguayans

24. FEDEFAM The Latin American Federation of Associations of the Families of the Detained-Disappeared

25. FUNDALATIN Latin American Foundation for the Defense of Human Rights andSocial Development

26. CAL The Argentine Committee for Liberty

27. IADH Latin American Institute for Human Rights

28. ILDIS Latin American Institute for Social Research

29. SIJAU International Secretariat of Jurists for Amnest in Uruguay

30. SELADEH Latin American Human Rights Secretariat

31. TySAE Argentine Workers and Trade Unionists in Exile